And the Next Question is

......powerful questions for sticky moments

(Revised Edition)

Rachel A. Alexander & Julia M. L. Russell

A coaching resource for all coaches and those engaged in a coaching-style of managing.

Paperback ISBN 978-1-78705-266-6

ePub ISBN 9781-1-78705-267-3

PDF ISBN 978-1-78705-268-0

Published in the UK by MX Publishing

335 Princess Park Manor, Royal Drive, London, N11 3GX

www.mxpublishing.com

Cover design by Brian Belanger

Rachel - this book is dedicated to all those yet to tick off their number one thing on their bucket list – get out there and do it! Second time around is just as good as the first time I ticked that particular box!

Julia - this book is dedicated to June, Roy, Mark, Cheryl & Margie - resting forever in my heart; and to Ivan - my inspiration and future.

Praise for
'And the Next Question Is...'

'It is rare to find a book which combines such considerable experience with substantial depth of knowledge, as 'And the Next Question Is...'. Not only is it a unique and invaluable resource and an expertly curated series of questions, it is also an extensive vocabulary for new coaches. In addition, it provides an inspiration for experienced coaches, leaders and managers. I consider it to be essential reading, and one of the most powerful books in the coaching armoury, and I would not hesitate in recommending 'And the Next Question is...' for your library'
Gina Lodge CEO
Academy of Executive Coaching (AoEC)

'Julia and Rachel have put together a unique book of powerful questions that could be of help to coaches at all levels of experience. I believe it will be especially useful to coaches just starting out in the profession because it will deal with the recurring question of 'What do I say now?' I applaud Julia and Rachel for having the wisdom and courage to do something as unusual as this book'
Ed Modell – PCC Coach & Past President
International Coach Federation

'This book is a fabulous resource and the questions it contains will be helpful in life and work, and it's now refreshed and better than ever. As one of Rachel's coaching clients I've often been tempted to pause the session and write down her amazing, insightful questions rather than stay fully present and answer. Now I can turn to 'And the next question is' and its perceptive, sensitive questions in my own time. This book will help my own reflective practice, and will be useful to other non-coaches whether as a leader or a manager of people and teams'
Liz North - Director of External Affairs
Medical Membership Organisation

'Asking powerful questions in the right way, at the right moment, is an art and what makes coaching so powerful. As a fledgling coach, I can remember wracking my brains for a good question during many a coaching session – not the best way to be fully present! This book provides a raft of excellent questions to dip into and experiment with'
Deborah Price - Professional Certified Coach (ICF)

Contents

FOREWORD

The attribute that often distinguishes an outstanding coach, manager, or leader (from those who are just average) is their ability to ask powerful questions. Good questions do many different things. They can open up a rich conversation. They can promote clarity. They can fuel motivation. What often happens, though, is that we think of a powerful question an hour or a day after an important conversation took place.

If only there were a handy reference, like a book full of questions organized by topic. If there were such a thing, then before an important meeting or conversation, you could go to the relevant section of the book and read through a variety of powerful questions. You could tuck the most memorable or relevant ones in the back of your mind. Then during the interaction, you would be ready with questions that make a real contribution to everyone's thinking.

Or you might have a topic of your own that you want to resolve or gain more clarity about. You could pick up that reference book, and ask yourself a question. You could even let synchronicity choose a question for you. You could open the book and point your finger, then ask yourself the question you pointed to.

I think Rachel and Julia were wishing for such a resource, but they couldn't find one, so they had to create it themselves. The volume before you, now in its second edition, is the result.

This is one of those books that you will keep pulling off your shelf. It is clearly organized and packed full of the kinds of questions that promote change, whether it be change in our thinking or perspective, in our commitments, or even in our sense of who we are as a person.

We consciously craft a life, a project, or a career when we ask ourselves relevant questions, and then dig deeply within to find the answers that are right for us. Over time, questioning becomes a habit. You actively choose your life, rather than just having it happen to you.

Incrementally, this process of inquiry can lead to fulfilment in your life, excellence in your projects, and satisfaction in your career. Your questions of others promote enhanced relationships and rich collaborations.

So, ask away. You just happen to have a book in your hands, or on your device, that will help you do that.

Jan Elfline
EdD, MCC

Jan Elfline began coaching in 1993 and was one of the first to be recognized as a Master Certified Coach (MCC) by the International Coach Federation. From 1998 to the present she has taught coaching in North America, Europe and Asia. Her training organization, Aligned Action International, combines the language tools and thinking strategies of Neuro-Linguistic Programming (NLP) with the practice of coaching.

Introduction

Contents

Since the first edition was published in 2012 we have listened attentively to feedback. It became apparent that additional chapters were needed to cover topics we were seeing more in our active coaching businesses. So, in addition to what evolved as a complete rewrite / edit, we added a chapter on Lifestyle and Wellbeing and Business Development and Change Management (under Influence). We have also added further suggested reading and resources at the end of the book.

A great question is more valuable than a good answer. We invite you to look through these pages, find the right question for the moment and ask that powerful question which will unleash the innate wisdom in all of us. Read on...

Objectives of the book

This is a working collaboration between two professional coaches whose objective is to reach out to more people, make a difference and contribute to the coaching profession by sharing knowledge through a published piece of work. **'And the next Question is ...'** a very practical and easy to use book, which we hope will form part of every coach's essential toolkit as it enables you to easily find key questions in some of the most distinctive areas of coaching, such as confidence, leadership, communications, balance and life-purpose.

What this book is/is not

This book can be used in a number of ways; as a memory jogger for experienced coaches, a reference or resource tool for the new coach, a trigger to send you off exploring on a quest of your own or a way to prepare for a coaching session by flicking through the pages and seeing what grabs your attention. You could also use this book to focus on a particular chapter which you believe may help your client, to gain inspiration or as an escape in those 'sticky' moments when one's mind goes blank.

What this book is not is an exhaustive or a priority list of all the questions one might need in a coaching session. It is a list of questions which we have created or gathered during more than 15 years of practical professional coaching experience, research and feedback from clients and colleagues alike and which we would like to share with a wider community.

These questions have helped us in 'sticky moments' when we have thought *'what could be the next really great question I could ask?' or 'Help, what do I say next?!'* Sometimes the answer may be *'Nothing'*; silence is golden (to coin a phrase) and often enables the client to find their own answer and sometimes another question for themselves. However, if something does come or needs to be said it is our hope that the following pages provide some assistance in finding the question that makes the difference, or moves you / your client on, maybe even that 'killer question' or what we prefer a 'powerful question'.

How to read/use this book

This book has been constructed as a reference or resource book. It is divided into chapters and at the beginning of each chapter is a guide as to the contents of that chapter, listed in alphabetical order for ease of reference. At the start of each section is a shaded area which provides our definition of that particular topic and any important points that we feel would enhance your experience of that section. The questions are then listed, in no particular order, although sometimes, you may find there is a flow or sequence to the questions, which you may or may not follow as is your wish. Some questions may appear similar and it is our way of providing alternatives as they may feel different / elicit a different response when asked in a different context. We also thought it important to replicate some questions as not all questions are mutually exclusive to any one chapter.

The questions are numbered to enable you to refer back to a particular question at a later date, select a few of your favourites and be able to pinpoint them 'in the moment' with ease later on.

Also, you will occasionally find a blank page, entitled 'My Favourite Questions', to allow you to write your own notes or add further powerful questions, which may have been triggered during reading the questions on the previous pages.

Following is an example of how the layout has been constructed:

Beliefs

Beliefs are the principles / rules / assumptions that guide our actions, they are our reality and we act upon them. Questions that challenge them can cause change - moving the client forward into a different, more positive action or place.

1. What do you believe about time? [e.g. time is money, there is never enough time etc.]
2. What is really important to you about time?

Within some questions you will find an 'X'. The intention is that where this appears the client's own words are to be used within the question. For example:

1. What has to happen before X?
2. If you did more of X what would you get from this?

This book can be used across all of the different ways of coaching. In telephone coaching it can sit on the desk alongside the coach and provides easy access to questions 'in the moment' by flicking through the pages. For face-to-face coaching, it could be used to get into the right frame of mind prior to the session starting, to cherry pick some new questions to retain in a client folder specific to that session/client or as a revision/learning aid. The questions could also be used for team coaching in a workshop environment by choosing those pertinent to the topic under discussion.

Who it is for and why will it be useful?

This book is a significant resource aimed at the following:

- New coaches to develop their collection of questions as they develop and grow as coaches.
- Experienced coaches as a refresher of questions which they may have used in the past and forgotten, as a memory jogger, to provide variety and stretch them to step out of their comfort zone
- External coaches
- Internal coaches
- Managers and leaders who use coaching skills within their business or company.
- Individuals who want to use a coaching style to develop people in a non- business organisation or to self-coach.

In fact, anyone and everyone who has an interest in asking questions as a means of developing, growing or improving themselves, their team or organisation and comes across those 'sticky moments' when the mind goes blank, your flow stops and you reach for this book. You flick through the pages and the perfect question pops out at you. You ask it and are back into your flow with yourself, your client or whomever you are with. This book has been written because a need was identified. We had been collecting, and sharing, questions for some time and there was no one place where we could go to find a large quantity of useful and powerful questions covering a number of common issues/topics which we had come across in our coaching sessions with clients. Our hope is that this continues to be a major resource to the coaching and business community, hence our decision to update and add new chapters.

About the Authors

Both Rachel and Julia are Professional Certified Coaches accredited by the International Coach Federation (ICF) and follow the code of ethics and coaching competencies as set out by the ICF. Coaching has now become well known and there are many different forms and models of coaching. The ICF defines coaching as *partnering with clients in a thought-provoking and creative process that inspires them to maximize their personal and professional potential'.*

In addition, we would like to add that to us coaching is not just focused at the behavioural level; it also covers generative change at all levels and is about helping people effectively achieve their outcomes. Our coaching is, mainly non-directive and incorporates many different models from the coaching world. The essential elements for us at all times are to be fully present with the client, always to demonstrate flexibility and remain with the client's agenda, whichever way that twists and turns.

How we came to write this book

Rachel – Since studying psychology in 6th form and later as part of my degree, I have been fascinated by how and why people operate as they do, but it was only when I began to lead teams that I really began to focus this fascination in the practical world. As I trained to be a professional coach I was aware of the number of books written and published concerning coaching – also the number of books that I seemed to buy, but barely dipped into and that at the end of the day the most used and useful 'book' I had was one I had created myself. The 24 pages of Powerful Questions I had compiled was not only a great tool for scanning prior to a coaching call to get me into the right frame of mind, but it was also the right resource, especially when I was a novice coach – available at the right time i.e. during a coaching call – if I needed some inspiration to help my client move forward.

I knew this tool was right for me and I felt strongly it was something that would be right for other coaches too. There was nothing similar on the market that I could find. The idea took shape - this was the book, as early as I could remember that I would like to write – with someone who felt as passionately as I did – enter my co-author, Julia.

Julia - My journey started as a 4-year-old growing up in Africa where my love of books and words developed and grew by feeding my imagination and love of exploration, adventure and travel. I have always been fascinated by language, how different people connect and communicate. Throughout a long career in finance and business travelling the world; asking questions, listening to the answers and gathering information was a common theme.

After leaving the corporate world to set up an international coaching business I had become known, during my training, as the research expert by dint of the number of books I had on all manner of topics. I was often contacted for information, help with a tricky situation or just to bounce ideas off. From the beginning, I had also started collecting powerful questions as a way of embedding the learning along the journey and shared some with colleagues. Throughout my life people have come along who have been significant in accompanying me on my journey; who have shared my values, provided encouragement and seen some potential – Rachel is one of those people and we had reached that point in the road together which said – write that book!

Acknowledgements

We would like to acknowledge our many coaching colleagues, clients, trainers, 'influencers' and the ICF in our coaching journey over the last 15 years. They have fed our love of questions and in particular Jan Elfline who has provided training and education, plus guidance and much encouragement for many years and told us to just get on and do it!

Our special thanks go to all those who reviewed our work and supported us along the way as this revised version developed. In particular the following, who spent an inordinate amount of time reviewing the book in its entirety - Ivan Waters, Jacqui Alexander and Ella Jaczynska.

Chapter 1
Client – Session Management

Contents

1st Coaching Session

These questions reflect the need to build the foundations of the coaching relationship and explore the reality of your client's world.

1. What is currently impossible for you to do that, if it were possible, would change everything?
2. How will you let me know if we are getting into territory you would rather stay out of?
3. What is your personal goal for our time together?
4. What do you think this experience might teach you?
5. How might the learning you get from this experience help you in the future?
6. How will stretching in this way develop your abilities?
7. What do you want to notice while you are taking this action?
8. What could we work on that would make the biggest difference to you?
9. What is the biggest challenge in your life today?

10. How will you know you were successful?

11. What is it about coaching that will make it a good fit for you?

12. Would you like me to ask you about that?

13. Are you choosing the life you live?

14. How will you choose to live your life instead?

15. How will you treat yourself well during our coaching?

16. If you thought of yourself as the majority stakeholder in your life – how does that change things?

17. What would be 100% right now?

18. What will you say 'YES' to?

19. What will you say 'NO' to?

20. What strategic decisions will help the system flourish into the next decades?

21. How would dwelling in reality, not possibility, cause a difference?

22. How would dwelling in possibility, not reality, cause a difference?

23. What has to happen before 'X'?

24. What do you want instead?

25. How do you want to use me as your coach?

26. What do you know about what motivates you?

27. What help do you need to move quickly towards your goals?

28. Do you want me to hold you accountable to take action?

29. What might you achieve if you committed to in-between assignments?

30. What is working for you?

31. What is not working for you?

32. What might you want to change?

33. What additional resources will move you forward?

34. How will you want to use me in this area?

35. What is the real issue?

36. What makes this an issue now to you / to others?

37. Who owns this issue / problem?

38. How important is it on a scale 1 – 10?

39. How much energy do you have for a solution on a 1 – 10 scale?

40. What would increase your energy?

41. What have you already tried?

42. If you could imagine this problem has already been solved - what would you see, hear, feel?

43. What are you currently doing to get in your own way?

44. What enables you to be really present?

45. What interferes with you being really present?

46. What is it like for you to be really present?

47. How would you like to use this time now in the present?

48. Where will you try and get me to give you feedback?

49. Where will you get slippery with me?

50. How will I know you are avoiding an issue?

51. What would be the most valuable topic to focus on?

52. What topic are you hoping I won't bring up?

53. What do you perceive threatens your peace?

54. What do you perceive threatens you / your work / business?

55. What do you perceive threatens your personal fulfillment?

56. What does all this mean for you?

57. In summing up this first session for you, how would you describe it has been for you?

58. When will we know it is enough?

Accountability

Is about having your clients account, without blame or judgment, for what they said they were going to do.

59. What will you do?
60. When will you do it?
61. What will you do to monitor your progress?
62. On a scale of 1 to 10 how likely are you to do these actions?
63. What will you need to know, to know that you have achieved it?
64. What milestones will you set up?
65. How will you know you're on track?
66. How often will you check you're on track?
67. What do you believe got in the way of achieving what you said you would do?
68. How will you report back to me when you have taken this challenging step?
69. What resources could you begin to explore before our next session?
70. What do you already have?
71. Where will you find the resources you need?
72. What is going to help you stay on track?
73. What would help you remember to do this?
74. What kind of structure would serve you?
75. How can this structure work better for you?
76. How do you want to track your progress with this task?
77. What support do you need from me to take the action you want to take?
78. How will you record your progress?

79. Who else can you enlist to support your agreed outcomes / coaching accountabilities?
80. What has enabled you to stay on track in the past?
81. What important learning might come out of taking this action?

Beginning a Session

These questions enable you, and your client, at the beginning of a session to set the context and focus on the outcomes they want to achieve during that particular session.

82. When you leave this coaching session, how would you like things to be for you?
83. How do you want to spend our time together?
84. What are you hoping for from this session?
85. Where do you want to focus your attention today?
86. What is your agenda for this session?
87. Where do you want to start?
88. What would you like to have happen by the end of this session?
89. What is the most important thing that you and I should be talking about today?
90. What has become clear since we last met?
91. How did you get on with the actions from the last session?
92. What did you achieve by doing them?
93. [*If they didn't achieve them*] - what got in your way?
94. How was it completing the in-between assignments?
95. Has anything else come up we need to discuss since you sent me your agenda / prep form?

End of Each Session Debrief

> Rounding off a coaching session with a series of reflective questions allows the client to integrate / consolidate.

96. What stood out for you in our session today?
97. If you could capture your learning from this session in three or four words, what would they be?
98. What do you take away from our conversation that will influence your actions?
99. How will you use it?
100. When you reflect on our time in this session, what do you notice?
101. What is the learning from today?
102. What did you notice about your process as we were working together?
103. What, if any, ideas do you have about how this task was accomplished?
104. What future changes have come out of your learning?
105. What did you enjoy?
106. What was successful?
107. What was easy?
108. What would you like more of?
109. What would you like less of?
110. Where might you have dug deeper into what was really going on?
111. What would have really stretched you?
112. How will you make time to achieve your accountabilities before our next session?
113. What method would you like to use to report back to me?

114. What would you need to do between now and the next session to make it even more impactful for you?
115. On a scale of 1 – 10, how much closer did you move towards your outcomes?
116. What would you like to do before our next appointment that would move you forward on your outcomes?
117. Do you have an enquiry / question that you would like to ponder before our next meeting?
118. What more can I do to assist you?
119. What do you want to take away from this session?
120. What are you grateful for?
121. Did you do your best today?
122. What can you do better tomorrow?
123. What are you going to achieve tomorrow?
124. What is your intention as you leave this session?
125. What will that get you?
126. Where will this lead?
127. What are the chances of success?
128. What is your prediction?
129. Is there anything else you want to add to this subject or are we done?

Final Session

This session is a time for integration, consolidation and reflection of the whole coaching programme.

130. What themes have we covered?
131. How does this piece fit into the whole?
132. How is this similar to other experiences you have had?
133. How is this dissimilar to other experiences?

134. What does this learning build upon?

135. How does this fit with your values?

136. What is the learning from this experience?

137. How do you make sense of this?

138. Now that we have concluded our coaching what accountability / action would be appropriate?

139. How would you now describe where we started?

140. What patterns did you notice?

141. What worked that you want to continue with?

142. Where will all this take you?

143. What will you do differently?

144. How will you teach / instruct others to work with you?

145. What have others told you that they have noticed?

146. How do you now want to work with colleagues / family?

147. What behaviour changes have you noticed?

148. What was the single most important change?

149. What are the most valuable ideas and techniques you have received from this coaching programme?

150. How will you strengthen and maintain your gains from coaching?

Personal Strategies

This section focuses on more in-depth questions relating to how your client operates (also see page 178)

151. What strategy do you have to make the changes you would like to?

152. If you've identified a clear direction, do you feel on track?

153. How do you get from where you are to where you want to be?

154. If you did more of 'X' what would you get from this?

155. What is the pay-off of being where you are now?

156. What would you need in order to create a clear direction?

157. What do you need to do to feel on track?

158. What would you like to commit to - that you're really clear about?

159. What requires immediate attention?

160. Is it all right for us to go further with this issue?

161. How receptive are you to hearing a hard truth?

162. How receptive are you to others commenting on your behaviour?

163. What speed would you like to travel at with coaching?

164. How will you let me know if we are getting into territory you would rather stay out of?

165. What is the underlying pattern that you have observed?

166. Is there anywhere you would rather we didn't go?

167. What would be the most important topic to focus on right now?

168. By undertaking this coaching, what will be different for you?

169. What is the bottom-line of the current situation?

170. What could we work on right now that would really put a smile on your face?

171. What makes this a good time to make a commitment to achieving your goals?

172. If money was not a consideration, how would you live your life?

173. What thoughts are going through your mind in this particular situation?

174. What would you like to do / focus on first?

175. What is the clear and specific goal you would like to achieve?

176. What could you do?

177. What would you really like to do?

178. What is out of harmony?

179. What do you do to restore it?

180. If you couldn't fail, what would you do?

181. What can you do now to create that reality?

182. What issues could this create for you?

183. How will you tell this story in the future?

Ponderings (aka Enquiries)

> This section provides open-ended questions should you want to give the client something to take away and ponder in-between the sessions. Sometimes called enquiries.

184. What is 100% for you in life / work / relationships?

185. What is it to have a full, rich life?

186. What is integrity?

187. How do you operate?

188. What is your prevalent mood?

189. When you think about your prevalent mood – is it a habit?

190. What is choice?

191. What is it to choose?

192. Are you being nice or are you being real?

193. Where is your attention? (*On self, others, work, daydreams, vision*)

194. What keeps you going?

195. What frees you up?

196. Where are you too hard on yourself?

197. What is present when you are at your best?
198. When are you unable to laugh at yourself?
199. Who are you becoming?
200. What motivates you?
201. What is it to be creative?
202. What is it to be tenacious?
203. What is it to be passionate?
204. Where might you have withheld yourself from a compelling future?
205. Is what you are doing, right now, life affirming or life numbing?
206. What is the lie?
207. Where do you give your power away?
208. Who do you give your power to?
209. When do you give your power away?
210. What are your false assumptions?
211. What do you pretend (to know or not to know)?
212. What do you need to leave alone?
213. Where are you an automatic 'NO' or 'YES'?
214. Where do you limit yourself?
215. What is it to move towards the fear?
216. Where are you selling out on yourself?
217. Where are you uncompromising?
218. Where are you too flexible?
219. What are you unwilling to risk?
220. What is it to be grateful?
221. What will recharge your batteries?
222. What is fun?
223. How can you contribute to your reserves of fun / balance / resourcefulness?

224. How can you have this be easy?

225. What is grace / serenity?

226. What truly makes you laugh?

227. Do you choose heavy or do you choose light?

228. What is abundance?

229. How can this be playful and light?

230. When will you take a break today?

231. What is it to be generous with yourself today?

232. What do you regret?

233. What are you unwilling to change?

234. Where are you taking your foot off the gas?

235. What decision have you been avoiding?

236. Where do you stop short?

237. What are you being right about?

238. What are you settling for?

239. What are you overlooking?

240. How do you sabotage yourself?

241. What do you expect of yourself?

242. What is it to be proactive?

243. What is it to be fluid / flexible?

244. What is completion?

245. Where are you incomplete?

246. Who have you become?

247. What have you learned about yourself?

248. What is momentum?

249. What acknowledgement would you like to give yourself?

250. What do you consider beyond your ability?

251. What would be a stretch for you?

252. What makes you think anything is beyond you?

253. What would happen if you tried it?

254. How could you raise the bar for yourself?

255. What would be an even bigger goal?

256. What is the highest you could aspire to?

257. What would you aspire to do if you hadn't set a limit?

Reality Check (With a Balance Wheel)

Questions to assist your client, when they have completed a coaching balance wheel, by taking a snap shot of how satisfied they are with their current work / life right now.

258. How satisfied are you with the current state of balance?

259. How fulfilled is your life right now?

260. What struck you when you viewed your balance wheel?

261. What do you notice as you look at your wheel?

262. What surprises you about it?

263. What segment needs urgent attention?

264. Which sections are too small?

265. If each section were marked as 10 / 10 what would it look like / feel like?

266. If you could take one action what would it be?

267. What would you like to change?

268. What could you do to change this?

269. What would that do for you?

270. How would changing a section make a difference?

271. When any section is the right size, how does it enhance what is going on in all the other sections?

272. Specifically, how does it impact the whole wheel?

273. What sections, if any, benefit disproportionately?

274. What do you want to do to prioritise these?

275. What else are you willing to explore in creating balance for yourself?
276. Which section requires immediate attention?
277. If you changed one section where would you derive the greatest benefit with the least amount of effort?
278. What actions could change more sections of the wheel?
279. Who else could be impacting the balance of your wheel?
280. What trade-offs are you willing to make?
281. What difference will that make?

Values

These questions elicit what is truly important to your client. They are unique to your client, the qualities that define them and help them make choices. Values relate to principles rather than morals and are why we do what we do.

282. What is important to you?
283. What is important to you about work / relationships?
284. What is it about that, which makes it important?
285. When did you decide that that was important to you?
286. What do you really care about?
287. What really matters to you?
288. What incredible / peak moments have you had?
289. What makes them so special?
290. What emotions were happening at that time?
291. What really annoys you?
292. What is it about that which causes you to feel that way?
293. What actions are most aligned with your values?
294. Are you living your most important values now, in the present?

295. What would you need to be doing differently?

296. What bits are missing?

297. What would your top five values be?

298. What do you want to change or improve upon in order to be more congruent with your values?

299. As you look at each of your most important values, are they moving you towards what you want or away from what you don't want?

300. How will you know the difference?

301. If you had all your values present in your work, what would make you leave it?

302. What is it that makes you feel really motivated?

303. What happens to you that lets you know you're motivated?

304. What needs to be present to be motivated?

305. What is really at stake in living your values?

Year-end Review

A series of questions that will enable your client to reflect, take the learnings and focus on the future, leaving the past behind.

306. What lessons have you learned this past year?

307. What do you need to stop, start and / or change in the year ahead?

308. What reasons do you have for doing these things?

309. What New Year resolutions have you made in the past that you have stuck to?

310. What made you be successful with them?

311. What got in your way?

312. Who can support you as you plan these new changes?

313. What would be a positive way of framing your New Year resolutions?
314. What could prevent you from achieving them?
315. How will you know you have been successful?
316. What small, incremental steps could you create?
317. How will you reward your success in the coming year?
318. What will you let go of to be successful?
319. How will you reward yourself for your success?
320. What are you grateful for in the last year?
321. What is the one thing you would have done differently?
322. What will make this coming year the best yet?
323. What will you take forward with you from the last year into next year / this coming year?

Chapter 2
Goals and Outcomes

Contents

Commitment

Questions to evaluate your clients desire to achieve their stated goals and outcomes.

1. When is commitment easy for you?
2. When have you committed to something?
3. What was required?
4. What were your actions?
5. What are the strategies you can use now?
6. How would that look / feel / sound?
7. What are you truly committed to?
8. What are you now ready to commit to?
9. What are the options for action here?
10. What criteria will you use to judge the options?
11. Which option seems the best one against those criteria?
12. Which one seems the worst?
13. How would someone you really admire handle this situation?
14. What options do you believe there are?
15. Which one would add the most value?
16. What could be the effects of taking this action?
17. What is needed to make this work?

18. What could you do to make this work?

19. What personal strengths / resources do you bring?

20. What are you committed to actually doing?

21. What makes you confident that you can pull this off?

22. What is the first step?

23. When will that happen?

24. How will you keep track of your successes?

25. What is important about this story?

26. What did you learn from that experience?

27. What will you do?

28. How will you do that?

29. What change is worth making?

30. Are you committed to making a change?

31. What will get you started?

32. What kind of plan do you want to make?

33. What action could you take to improve this situation?

34. Do you have what it takes to make this work?

35. What will be different when you have your solution?

36. What will increase your commitment?

37. On a scale of 1 – 10 how committed are you to taking action?

38. How will you report back to me?

Distractions

> We define a distraction as being something that takes your client's attention away from forwarding their actions.

39. I'm really interested in your story, I also want you to get the most from our time - is this the best use of our time?

40. What can you distil from this incident?

41. What is the bottom line?

42. What is the learning from what happened?

43. What will you remember about this in ten years time?

44. I sense you are avoiding something, what is the truth?

45. What are you unwilling to address?

46. What is the lie to yourself / others?

47. How long do you want to repeat this pattern?

48. What serves you in this pattern?

49. So let me stop you there – what is the essence of this?

50. How much time and energy are lost to distractions?

51. What are the typical distractions in your work environment?

52. What are the typical distractions at home?

53. How could you diminish distractions in either of these environments?

54. What would be the benefit?

55. How committed are you to taking action to limit these distractions?

56. What will you do?

57. What would be an appropriate time frame for you doing this?

58. What is the fear that is causing this distraction?

59. What distracts you most?

60. What do you fear most?

61. What major fear will you be addressing if you 'X'?

62. What 'magic solution' would make that fear decrease?

63. What would make it disappear?

64. How often is worry in your thoughts?

65. How does it show itself?

66. Where else could energy for this change come from?

67. Will this action lead to happiness?
68. What gets in the way?
69. What follows this behaviour?
70. How will you behave differently?
71. What is the worst thing that could happen if you did 'X'?
72. What is the best thing that could happen if you did 'X'?
73. What is the worst thing that could happen if you didn't do 'X'?
74. What is the best thing that could happen if you didn't do 'X'?
75. What reason did this story come into our coaching session?
76. Give me the golden nugget that you mined from this experience?
77. On a scale of 1 – 10 how committed are you to reducing your distractions?
78. What needs to happen to get it to a 10?

Goal Planning

The art of planning for desired results. Creating goals assists the client to know where they wish to end up and how the journey will manifest itself.

79. How will you know you reached your goal?
80. What would be a good goal for you?
81. How would this goal be aligned with your values?
82. Who else shares this goal?
83. What do you need to do?
84. How could you make this into smaller steps?
85. What are the parts of this task?

86. How can you isolate some pieces that will move you towards your goals?

87. What small step would get you started?

88. What would be an easy first bit?

89. What else do you want?

90. What other choices do you have?

91. What will this goal get you?

92. What is important to you about this?

93. What are you willing to give up / let go of to accomplish this?

94. What are you willing to change?

95. What were you trying to achieve when you did that?

96. Where have you previously been successfully with changes?

97. What can you learn from this?

98. What will you do differently next time?

99. What is good about this present situation?

100. What can you do to make a difference?

101. What could be stopping you from taking action?

102. What goal would you like to begin with?

103. Can you do that today?

104. What would you have to do first?

105. How would that happen?

106. Is that in line with your goal?

107. How would that be for you?

108. What would be the cost to you of doing this?

109. What would be the opportunity missed?

110. What would help you remember to do this?

111. What kind of structure would serve you?

112. How can this structure work better for you?

GROW Model Questions

A simple yet powerful framework for structuring a session. Developed from the Inner Game theory developed by Timothy Gallwey and a significant contribution was made by Sir John Whitmore.

113. **Goal** – what do you want?
114. **Reality** – where are you now?
115. **Options** – what could you do?
116. **Will** – what will you do?

Goal

117. How long will this goal take?
118. When do you want the goal?
119. How long is needed to achieve it?
120. What will you see, hear, and feel?
121. Who are you being when 'X'?
122. Is this goal under your control?
123. What are you going to do?
124. What can you offer others so they'll help?
125. How will you measure feedback?
126. How often will you measure progress?
127. What are the consequences?
128. What is the cost of going for this goal?
129. What is the cost of not going for this goal?
130. What is the time needed to achieve the goal?
131. What opportunity may be opened up for you?
132. What opportunities might you be losing by going for this?
133. What might you give up?

134. How will the balance between different aspects of your life be affected?
135. What will you leave behind that is important now?
136. What is it you would like to discuss?
137. What is the aim of this discussion?
138. What do you want to achieve in the long term?
139. What do you want to do instead of 'X'?
140. Is that realistic?
141. How do you know this goal is worth achieving?
142. How will you know when you have achieved it?
143. What will you see, hear and feel when you have achieved it?
144. What does success look like?
145. How much personal control or influence do you have over your goal?
146. What would be a milestone on the way?
147. By when do you want to achieve it?
148. Is that positive, challenging and attainable?
149. How will you measure it?

Reality

150. If you were to focus only on facts - what is happening right now?
151. How do you know this is accurate / true?
152. When, where and how often does this happen?
153. Who is directly involved?
154. Who is indirectly involved?
155. If things are not going well with this issue, who else gets drawn in?
156. What happens to you?

157. How do you feel?

158. What about others involved, what happens to them?

159. What is their perception of the situation?

160. What have you done about this so far?

161. With what results?

162. How often have you tried?

163. What is missing in this situation?

164. What is holding you back from a way forward?

165. How has that served you so far?

166. What is really going on here?

Options

167. What makes you think you don't have a choice?

168. What approaches have you seen in similar situations?

169. What options do you have for steps to resolve this issue?

170. What could you do?

171. What else might you do?

172. What would you do differently if you were able to start again?

173. Who might be able to help?

174. What would someone who handles this kind of issue really do well?

175. What if you had more time for this issue, what might you try?

176. What is the right thing to do?

177. What is the most courageous step to take?

178. If the constraints were removed what would you do?

179. What if you had less time?

180. What might that force you to try?

181. Image that you had more energy and confidence, what could you do then?
182. What if somebody said, 'Money no object!' What might you try then?
183. If you had total power, what might you try then?
184. What should you do?
185. Would you like another suggestion, if so who could give it?
186. What are the costs and benefits of each of these ideas?

Will

187. What are the next steps?
188. What option or options do you choose?
189. How will this address your goal?
190. To what extent does this meet all your objectives?
191. What are your criteria and measurements for success?
192. When, precisely, will you start each action step?
193. When, precisely, will you finish each step?
194. What could hinder you taking these steps?
195. What will it cost you if you don't take action?
196. What might get in the way?
197. Who needs to know?
198. What support do you need?
199. What would need to happen to enable you to ask them?
200. What could I do to support you?
201. On a scale of 1 – 10 how motivated are you?
202. What prevents this from being a 10?
203. What do you need to do to get your commitment up to 10?
204. What personal resistance do you have to taking these steps?

205. What will you do to eliminate these external and internal factors?
206. Is there anything else you want to talk about now, or are we finished?

Achievement and Obstacles

> We have defined this section as being questions that relate to moving your client forward. Obstacles being something that prevent your client from moving forward, something or someone that stands in the way.

207. What are you afraid of that you'd rather not be?
208. What do you want to forget?
209. What seems to be the trouble?
210. What seems to be the main obstacle?
211. What is stopping you?
212. What concerns you most about 'X'?
213. What do you want?
214. How can you get out of your own way?
215. What worries you about taking a different approach?
216. What is missing?
217. Imagine yourself 5 or 10 years from now. Looking back, how do you remember this day?
218. What do you want to remember?
219. What different decisions would you make?
220. What would happen if all obstacles magically disappeared?
221. What could you do if all the obstacles magically disappeared?
222. What will you do to start removing the obstacles?
223. Where did these barriers come from?

224. What might be preventing you from doing 'X'?

225. Imagine that money, time, skills were not an issue. What could stop you then?

226. What is the hesitation about getting started?

227. What is standing in your way?

228. What is the first step you can take to removing the obstacle?

229. When will you start this process?

230. What could hold you back in 'X' situation?

231. So, what is actually getting in the way of you doing this right now?

232. And if you did go through with this action, what is the worst that could happen?

233. What would you do if you weren't afraid?

234. What is the risk you could live with?

235. What are you afraid would happen?

236. How could you approach this situation if you weren't afraid of failing?

237. What would be the best way to tackle that fear / anxiety?

238. What are you doing now that gets in the way of what you want to achieve?

239. What do you understand about this situation?

240. What do you choose to do with that understanding?

241. What could you do to improve that?

242. Who may be available to help / support you in this?

243. If not you, then who?

244. If not now, then when?

245. What can you do differently?

246. How willing would you be to do your part to make that happen?

247. If nothing changes, what will that cost you?

248. What would be the result if you did 'X'?

249. What other resources (people or things) can you use to help you find the answer to your issue?

250. What do you want to do with this?

251. What is the next stage?

252. What do you have the power to do right now?

253. What would increase that power?

254. What is the smallest possible step you could take immediately, in the right direction?

255. So, what would have to happen for you to set it up that way?

256. What wouldn't have to happen?

257. What wouldn't happen if you didn't do 'X'?

258. What would you be losing if you did nothing?

259. What could you do today?

260. What would you do if you knew you couldn't fail?

261. Imagine that you can do anything, what would you do?

262. What is it that you want to achieve / accomplish?

263. If you could wave a magic wand...what would you change?

264. What is the best use of your time right now?

265. Who is in control?

266. Who decides the moves?

267. What would it take to move you toward 'YES'?

268. What does the road ahead look / feel like?

269. What road are you on?

270. What road calls to you?

271. What would / could be a decisive step?

272. How will you take that step-in spite of uncertainty?

273. What does this need to look like to make you feel comfortable with moving forward?
274. How important is it for you to find a solution for this issue?
275. What would be your first / next step / to move towards that solution?
276. What advice would you give someone else who is struggling with the same issue?
277. What if you were able to get past 'X'?
278. What do you see when you step back and see the whole picture?
279. If you were in a helicopter hovering above this situation; what do you notice?
280. What else do you see?
281. What is trying to emerge here?
282. What is happening now?
283. If you don't take yourself seriously, why should anyone else?
284. How would this decision affect others close to you?
285. What lesson can be learned from this?
286. Who could you talk to who could shine some light on this situation?
287. How many different ways can you think of to respond to this situation?
288. What is the value of your current attitude?
289. Has there ever been a time when 'X'?
290. What was it like?
291. What is stopping you from achieving your goal?
292. What resources do you need to help you decide?
293. What do you know about it now?
294. How do you suppose you can find out more about it?

295. What kind of picture do you have right now?

296. What resources are available to you?

297. What would reduce the impact of the obstacle?

298. What actions would assist that reduction?

Well-formed Outcome Planning

The outcome is always where your client is headed, it sets the direction for taking the appropriate actions. It focuses their attention on the ultimate aims. Detailed planning significantly increases the chances of success. The outcome being well formed enables your client to ensure all aspects have been considered.

299. What do you want?

300. What will it do for you?

301. How will you know when you've got it?

302. What will you be seeing when you've got it?

303. What will you be hearing when you've got it?

304. What will you be feeling when you've got it?

305. What will you be doing when you've got it?

306. What will others see you doing when you've got it?

307. What will others hear you saying when you've got it?

308. Can you start and maintain this outcome?

309. What else do you need to make it happen?

310. If you need support, what do you need to do to get that support?

311. When, where and with whom do you want it?

312. How long do you want it to last?

313. When, where and with whom do you not want it?

314. What are the benefits of the current situation?

315. How will you plan to maintain these?
316. What do you get out of your current behaviour that you want to keep?
317. Will this change be worth the cost to you, in terms of emotion, energy and / or money?
318. Will it be worth the investment of time?
319. Will this outcome be in keeping with who you are / your values?
320. What is standing in the way of an ideal outcome?
321. What evidence will you need to know that you are moving towards your outcome?
322. What do you really want – specifically?
323. How can you make it achievable?
324. How will things be different?
325. What do you want to focus on?
326. Will this require a behavioural change?
327. How will you know you are on track?
328. What control do you have to make it happen?
329. What are the strategies, talents and skills you have?
330. What are the resources you have to draw upon?
331. How do you want to use coaching to support your outcomes?
332. How do you want to use me to help you achieve this outcome?
333. Which outcome would be most valuable for you?

My Favourite Questions

Chapter 3
Communication

Contents:

Answers

> Questions to elicit answers from your client when they feel they do not have one!

1.   What is the simple answer?

2.   Let us suppose you did know what the answer was, how would you know when you found it?

3.   What would be different?

4.   If I could give you the answer to what you want right now, what would the question be?

5.   What would be the most powerful question I could ask you right now?

6.   What would be the most useful question for me to ask you next?

7.   What question do you hear me asking you right now?

8.   What do you want to say 'YES' to regarding how you communicate?

9.   What do you want to say 'NO' to regarding how you communicate?

10. What will you do now in order to do the 'YES' things

11. When do you compromise in your communication?

12. When is compromise appropriate?

13. When is compromise incongruent, out of alignment with who you are and what you believe in?

14. What is out of harmony?

15. What would you need to do to restore it?

16. What choices do you want to make in how you communicate?

17. If you had a friend / colleague who had this issue what would you say to them?

18. How could you change your style so that your listener truly understands?

19. What do you envisage reporting back to me when you have taken action?

20. What do you take away from our conversation that will influence your actions?

21. How open / available are you to hearing the answer?

Awareness

These are questions that stimulate the curiosity of the client to discover and learn more, often about themselves.
Awareness for the client generates choices.

22. What would good communication sound like?

23. What is the essence of this?

24. What is funny about this situation?

25. If you were looking for the humour what would you find?

26. What would it feel like to have a good laugh about this?

27. What do you really mean to convey?

28. What more can you say about this that others may hear?

29. What would be your bottom line?

30. What assumptions are you making in your communication?

31. What is the positive intention behind this behaviour?

32. What other ways are there of saying that?

33. What do you wish you had said?

34. What do you think others notice about your behaviour?

35. What do you think I have heard so far?

36. What do you need to say to make it happen?

37. What stops you being listened to?

38. What would positively stretch you now?

39. If it had been you, what would you have done?

40. How else could you handle this?

41. What kind of picture do you have right now?

42. What values are being expressed when you do this?

43. What is your favourite sound?

44. What does that sound mean to you?

45. How comfortable do you feel doing things alone?

46. How comfortable do you feel asking for help?

47. What does integrity mean to you?

48. How do you communicate that to others?

49. How do you know you're being realistic?

50. What would you need to add / change to be more realistic?

51. How does your enthusiasm show up in the way you communicate?

52. How well do you know your communication style?

53. What is your personal blueprint?

54. How can you make that blueprint more effective?

55. Who can assist you?

56. When will you put that into actions?

57. How well do you communicate your ideas to others?

58. How long do you want to repeat this pattern?

59. How would you describe your pattern?

60. What are you overlooking?

61. How do you sabotage yourself in your communications?

62. What could you do differently today?

63. Who would that impact most?

64. What will you gain?

Difficult Conversations

> This section is aimed specifically at assisting your client to identity their issues around having difficult conversations they want / need to have. Enabling them to put positive strategies in place for success.

65. What conversations do you need to have?

66. What is the outcome you want from this conversation?

67. What would happen if you had this conversation?

68. With whom should you be having this conversation?

69. Who else can assist you?

70. What are you unwilling to address?

71. What crucial conversations do you need to have to change the predicament?

72. With whom do you need to have those crucial conversations?

73. When will you be willing to ask the challenging questions?

74. What will these challenging questions be?

75. Who could champion you on this journey?

76. What would you be prepared to ask of them?
77. When will you make this ask?
78. What is it you would like to discuss?
79. What is the aim of this discussion?
80. What is actually being said right now?
81. What is the elephant in the room?
82. What is actually not being said?
83. How loudly are things not being said?
84. What is their perception of the situation?
85. How do you know their perception?
86. How does this differ from yours?
87. How could you make your communication clearer?
88. What unmet need would you like to articulate more clearly?
89. Who could shine some light on this situation?
90. How many different ways can you think of to respond to this situation?
91. What would you do now if you knew you could only gain from this conversation?
92. What is the worst thing that could happen if you said 'X'?
93. What is the best thing that could happen if you said 'X'?
94. What is the worst thing that could happen if you didn't say 'X'?
95. What is the best thing that could happen if you didn't say 'X'?
96. What question could you ask yourself right now?
97. What is the conversation you really need to have but haven't had so far?
98. What would happen if you did have it?
99. How can you make this easier for you?

100. How can you make this easier for others?

101. How can this be playful and light?

102. What new conversation can you start today to engage with those around you?

103. What communication have you been unwilling to hear from other people?

104. What conversations have you been deliberately avoiding having?

105. What difference could it make if you stop avoiding them?

106. What difficult conversations have you become resigned to?

107. What could make it a worthwhile or valuable conversation?

108. What is there that needs to be communicated, that hasn't been communicated?

109. What is there that wants to be communicated, that hasn't been communicated?

110. What is your intention going into this conversation and how might that influence the development of the conversation?

111. In having this conversation what aspects of your environment do you need to take into account?

Engaging with Draining People

Questions to challenge relationships that maybe toxic, draining of energy and pulling your client away from who they want to be.

112. What would happen if you stopped communicating with this person?

113. What is it that makes the relationship draining?

114. What purpose does this relationship serve?

115. How else might you get that?

116. What do you do to encourage them?

117. What could you do differently to discourage them?

118. How would it feel to know this individual was out of your life?

119. What would be a good way of expressing your difficulties to the person concerned?

120. What support / resources do you need to aid you in this communication?

121. How many hours in the next ten years will you continue to be drained by this person?

122. What is it costing you to be in this relationship?

123. How is that impacting on other relationships?

124. What kind of people would you rather spend time / communicate with?

125. What does this person bring out in you?

126. Who are you being when you are with this person?

127. How do they feed your insecurity / self-criticism / judgment of others / dishonesty?

128. What are you doing to ensure you spend valuable time with the people who bring out the best in you?

129. What are you doing to ensure you spend valuable time with the people who further your development?

130. Consider the value and attributes of people you like to spend time with, what would happen if you stopped seeing these people?

131. List 5 people you really admire (they can be current, passed away, known to you or people you would have liked to know) - what is it that you admire about them?

132. What do you need to say to them?

133. What can you cultivate in yourself that would enable you to choose different people to engage with?

Feedback

> Giving and receiving information that feeds the client forward into performance improvements or enables them to become more self-aware. Learning is always possible in the feedback (also see page 104).

134. What feedback would you give yourself?
135. What went well?
136. What caused it to go well??
137. What were your markers of success?
138. What went less well and why?
139. What will you do differently now?
140. What would you do the same way?
141. What would you like to do more of / less of?
142. What went unexpectedly well and why?
143. What went unexpectedly badly and why?
144. What, if any, new assumptions / rules have been made?
145. How could you have foreseen what happened?
146. What was your most important learning from this experience?
147. How can you improve learning in the future?
148. What would be a stretch for you?
149. Who will you enlist to support your stretch?
150. When will you put your new ideas into action?
151. What feedback would you like to give others?
152. What strategy will you use to ensure they hear and understand?

153. What would you need to do in order to maintain rapport and deliver difficult messages?

Note to coach: a great acronym for giving feedback[1]

154. S - in what **S**ITUATION did this occur?

155. A - what **A**CTIVITY was observed and by whom?

156. I - what **I**MPACT did this activity have?

157. L - what did it **L**EAD to / or what was the **L**EARNING from it?

Internal Negative Conversations

This section explores the internal world of your client, paying attention to the different 'characters' - sometimes known as gremlins (or saboteurs) that make up these silent internal conversations. Understanding our own gremlins is the first stage of dealing with them.

158. How is this internal dialogue / chatter / conversation serving you?

159. When do you notice your internal chatter?

160. What question do you have for yourself right now?

161. What conversation are you having with yourself?

162. Whose voice is it?

163. What do you want to tell them today?

164. What is your 'adult' message?

165. Who is really driving the bus here?

166. Who does your inner voice remind you of?

167. What does this little gremlin inside look like?

168. What name could you give this gremlin?

---

[1] *Feedback Model – S.A.I.L, courtesy of Jan Elfline (1998)*

169. What would happen if you changed the way it looked and sounded? *[Note to Coach: this could perhaps take the form of something fun e.g. a cartoon character with a silly voice, enabling them to take it less seriously]*

170. What actions can you take to quieten them?

171. What actions can you take to listen to them differently?

172. What actions can you take to interrupt them?

173. What do you need to say to this gremlin?

174. What is the positive intent of this gremlin for you?

175. What would happen if you could get that intent by doing something else?

176. What thoughts were going through your mind as you heard yourself say that?

177. What are the words inside your head when you think of this situation?

178. What are you saying to yourself about this?

179. Would you say those words to anyone else?

180. What part of you is really being hard on you?

181. Is this a problem that can be solved by thinking about it?

182. What else could you be thinking about?

183. How is this internal dialogue / chatter / conversation serving you?

184. How are your words to yourself making you feel?

185. What words would you rather hear?

186. How could you soften the sound?

187. Who is your harshest critic?

188. What would happen if you took control and put this internal critic into a quieter / smaller place?

Making an Impact

This section explores how your client makes their presence known and heard in addition to paying attention to others.

189. What would good communication sound like?
190. How do you 'show' up?
191. If a message is only as good as the response it gets – what response do you want?
192. So, how could you change your message to elicit the response you want?
193. When was the last time you made an impact?
194. What did you do that worked well?
195. What were you doing, saying, thinking, and feeling?
196. What will remind you of this time?
197. What are your key learnings?
198. What are the needs / outcomes of the others involved?
199. Who do you know that regularly makes an impact?
200. How do they make an impact?
201. What can you learn from them?
202. How will you get into the best possible frame of mind for this event?
203. What preparatory exercises / rituals work for you?
204. How will you position yourself to have the most impact?
205. If you are going to be on the phone will you sit down / stand up / move around?
206. What would taking a different position generate / do for you?
207. What do you know about the preferred style(s) of the other(s) involved?

208. How prepared are you to vary your language / approach to match this style?

209. What clear and concise opening sentence, that acknowledges your audience, have you planned?

210. How much of an impact can you make without words?

211. How can you engage with the other(s) involved?

212. What can you say to encourage yourself?

213. Where can you visualise yourself making an impact?

214. What will it be like when you've achieved your outcome?

215. How will you know that what you're doing is working?

216. How will you change your approach if you need to?

217. How will you remain centred, grounded and present?

218. Do you believe that you will make the biggest impact by just being yourself?

219. How might other people see it / see you?

220. If you feel that you can't - how would it be if you could?

221. What do you need to stop saying?

222. What do you need to start saying?

223. How big can your impact grow?

224. Who or what would benefit most if your impact were to shift?

225. Where would you most want to be noticed?

226. Who would you be, if you were more impactful?

Overwhelm

Overwhelm questions begin to assist your client to explore where they experience a sense of being overcome.

227. What requests will you make to eliminate this problem?

228. What is overwhelm for you?

229. What triggers that sense of overwhelm?

230. How does it build?

231. What actions will you do to eliminate this problem?

232. How can you practice saying 'NO'?

233. What do you notice about clear requests to you?

234. How can you practice making clear requests?

235. What patterns do you notice?

236. What themes emerge?

237. How can you express more of what you want in your every-day life?

238. How can you express what you want less of in your life?

239. What would it take to move you towards believing you can?

240. How can you choose to react differently?

241. How does how you are being, affect how / what you are communicating?

242. What are you experiencing / thinking / feeling about this situation?

243. What do you think he / she is experiencing / thinking / feeling in this situation?

244. What would you tell someone else in the same situation?

245. What habits create more stress for you?

246. What is the positive intent of choosing a hurried, tense way of being?

247. What else can you do to satisfy that positive intent?

248. Where are you creating stress through your thinking?

249. What other choice could you make?

250. What do you need to do to slow down?

251. What activities encourage a sense of peacefulness for you?

252. What is positive about the pace you are living at?

253. What is the cost to you and your family and friends of maintaining this pace?
254. What internal voices lead you to anxiety and overwhelm?
255. What can you do to begin to change them?
256. What causes you to feel a loss of control?
257. What would enable you to step back from this overwhelm?
258. What would you need to begin to do?
259. What will get you started?
260. What assistance will you need to get you started?

Presentations

Speaking in front of others is known to be one of our greatest fears – this section begins to explore how that fear can be minimised and how your client can become aware of what works or what needs changing in their own style.

261. What has been your presenting reality?
262. What are your biggest fears when making a presentation?
263. What would enable you to put these fears into a different perspective?
264. How could you overcome them?
265. How do these fears benefit you?
266. Who do you think is a really good presenter?
267. What is it that they do?
268. What would you need to do in order to 'model' some of their skills?
269. How could you use your voice and physiology differently?
270. Who is your audience expecting?
271. Who are you expecting to present?

272. What would make your presentation interesting to this audience?
273. What is the message you want to get across?
274. What are the three most important points of your message?
275. How could you be yourself while giving this presentation?
276. How could you make it more natural and authentic?
277. What feedback have you taken on board?
278. What do you notice about how you present?
279. What has anyone said to you about your presentations?
280. How could you speed up what you say?
281. How could you slow down what you say?
282. Where could be a good place to pause?
283. If this were an audience of teenagers would you hold their interest?
284. What is the purpose of your talk / presentation?
285. How will you physically represent your purpose?
286. How could you improve your presentation?
287. What do you need to change to make it flow more?
288. What do you want to know about your audience?
289. How will you be in the moment and adapt to your audience as your presentation goes along to?
290. What is the one question you don't want anyone to ask?
291. At which point in your presentation do you want to take questions?
292. How could you create more clarity in your presentation?
293. How do you need to be to appear fully confident?
294. What do you feel when you speak about your favourite subject?
295. If there is an issue, how would you handle it?

296. How will you know your audience is engaged?

297. How can you use the stage / lectern / screen to your benefit?

298. What is it you enjoy about speaking?

299. What will you do to ensure you demonstrate that?

300. Imagine you made the perfect presentation, what did you do differently?

301. How would I know it is perfect?

302. What will the praise feel and sound like?

303. What would happen if you acted 'as if' you are fully in control and enjoying it?

304. How could you 'bottle' that feeling?

Reflections and Ponderings

These questions enable the client to carefully consider where they are and where they want to be. These can generate useful information for moving forward. Some may also be useful for the client to take away and reflect on more deeply.

305. What questions should you ask yourself before our next meeting to make good use of our next coaching session?

306. How would you describe this situation / communication?

307. What changes do you need to initiate?

308. How will you initiate those changes?

309. What about the costs of changing – what are your plans to manage these?

310. What different story could you create about this situation?

311. What do people say about you after you have gone?

312. What would you like people to really say about you?

313. What needs to happen for you to create a mindset of success?

314. If you had 50% more confidence, how would that change how you communicate?

315. What is your body telling you?

316. What is your gut telling you?

317. How do you know that to be true?

318. What if the opposite were true?

319. What does this situation teach you about yourself?

320. How is this situation an opportunity for you to learn something really important?

321. How is that working for you?

322. What do you take that to mean?

323. What is right for you right now?

324. What else might be different?

325. What would that do for you?

326. What specifically could make this happen?

327. If you could do it over again, what would you do differently?

328. If you could do anything you wanted, what would you do?

329. What would it be like to be passionate in communications?

330. How could you find your voice?

331. What is it you want to tell the world?

332. Who do you most want to hear what you have to say?

333. What questions could you ask yourself before we next meet to hit the ground running at our next session?

334. Is that your heart or your head talking?

335. So, what would the other say?

336. Where are you communicating from - your head or your heart?

With Others

Interpersonal rapport and the ability to exchange words, thoughts and behaviours is the basis of communicating with others. This section explores that area.

337. What did you notice?
338. How could you have responded differently?
339. How did you feel when they said that to you?
340. What were the assumptions you made in what you heard?
341. What was their reaction to what you said?
342. How do others that you admire communicate differently from you?
343. What do you notice about their body language?
344. What do you notice about their tonality and tempo?
345. What specifically do they do that engages and influences?
346. What would you need to change that could assist you to model them?
347. How is that story working for you?
348. How will you know they have heard you?
349. How will you know your message has landed?
350. How can you communicate your vision to your team / organisation / family?
351. What is your communication strategy going to be?
352. What is the story you are buying into?
353. How do you know that you truly listen to others?
354. How do you choose to be in your communications today?
355. How do you perceive co-workers / family / friends?
356. How do you think they perceive you?
357. Was that a balanced exchange of views?

With Self

> This section explores your client's use of their internal dialogue in communicating with themselves.

358. What conversation are you having with yourself right now?

359. What resonates with you?

360. What is the outcome you want from this conversation?

361. How could you vary your behaviour to get a different result?

362. How could you say no to this request?

363. What are you afraid to say?

364. What needs to become clear for you?

365. What else could you do / say / think?

366. What are the words inside your head when you think of this situation?

367. What are you saying to yourself that you're not reacting to?

368. Would you say those words to anyone else?

369. What happens when you over think this?

370. What else could you be thinking about?

371. How are your words to yourself making you feel?

372. What story do you tell yourself?

373. If you were providing yourself with advice – what would you say to yourself right now?

374. How can you listen more to your inner wisdom?

375. What would make this true for you right now?

376. What if 'Why not' was the first question of every day?

377. What would happen if you followed your hunches?

378. How could you say what you think and still please yourself?

379. What do you want to accomplish in your communications today?
380. How do you know you are truly being listened to?
381. What would you need to say to yourself to create an empowering day?
382. What is your vision of how you see yourself in terms of your communication style?
383. What would enable you to have mastery in communications?

Chapter 4
Confidence

Contents:

Articulating What is Going On

> Articulating is the coach stating exactly what they are seeing, hearing and feeling concerning what the client has said. It can be the call to attention for the client stated as a statement of fact or an enquiring question.

1. How direct would you like me to be regarding what I see and hear in our sessions?
2. May I tell you a hard truth / observation?
3. Where would you rate your confidence on a scale of 1 – 10 as you discuss this?
4. What makes you feel most alive, this sounds draining?
5. What would raise your spirits, as this seems like you're lowering them?
6. What would bring you joy to put this in balance?
7. What will you find inspiring?
8. Who do you find inspiring?
9. What have you excelled at?
10. Where were you not so hot?
11. What have been your confidence highs / lows?

12. What key life events involving you / others have given you confidence?

13. What five achievements have made you feel good about yourself?

14. How has your confidence changed over time?

15. How is this affecting your confidence right now?

16. What do you have going for you right now?

17. Does having a lack of confidence mean you'll never do anything risky / adventurous again?

18. I'd like to explore further as 'X' seems to be getting in the way - would that be okay?

19. Is it alright for us to go further with this issue?

20. Can we devote more time to 'X'?

21. Where can we go in this area as this seems important?

22. What other choices do you have?

23. What is the real issue here?

24. What is behind this emerging pattern?

25. What is the bottom line?

26. What value was being violated / honoured?

27. What is the possible payoff for playing it safe?

28. What is the possible cost of playing it safe?

29. What is the potential payoff for being daring?

30. What is the potential cost of being daring?

31. What do you really want when this debris is cleared?

32. What I hear is you believe your options are reducing, so what other ideas / thoughts do you have?

33. What is the opportunity here?

34. What is the real challenge – the one you're avoiding?

35. How does this fit with your plans / way of life / values?

36. What do you think that means?

37. What is your assessment?

38. What is here that you want to explore?

39. Which part of the situation have you not yet explored?

40. What other angles can you think of?

41. What is just one more possibility?

42. What are your other options?

43. What is the real issue here?

44. Why is that an issue?

45. What is that issue costing you (in time, energy, money etc.)?

46. What is stopping you from doing something different?

47. What would need to happen to change this situation / issue?

48. How does it get in your way?

49. How are you getting in your own way?

50. What else happens because of this issue / situation that you're not mentioning?

51. What is the root cause of this as it seems you're skimming the surface?

52. What might happen if you don't do anything about it as you seem very stationary?

53. How many patterns do you notice as you tell this story?

54. This seems like a repeating theme – what else has yet to emerge?

55. How can you express more of what you want in your every-day life as the focus seems to be on what you don't want?

56. How can you choose to react differently as it seems you follow the same pattern?

57. Honest and open conversations don't seem to happen easily for you - what needs to change?
58. What is the real truth of the matter as many smoke screens are being presented?

Capability

This section suggests questions that could stretch the client to build new capabilities / skills, increasing their confidence to do things differently, better than before or even step outside their comfort zone.

59. What are your greatest capabilities?
60. What would make your best better?
61. What do you do that builds your capabilities?
62. What could you do that would increase your capabilities?
63. If you could be more confident what would that be like?
64. What kind of people do you spend time with?
65. How do they affect your learning and confidence to do something different?
66. How / why were you successful this past week?
67. What enabled you to be effective?
68. What specifically did you do?
69. How would you know you can't do it?
70. How confident are you that you believe that?
71. What can you learn from your past?
72. What do you feel capable of learning now?
73. What small steps would enable you to build your capability?
74. What is stopping you from doing this?
75. What would you do if you were ten times bolder?

76. When is experimenting more important that perfection?

77. Where would you like to stretch yourself?

78. When have you ever done anything like this before?

79. What happened when you did something similar?

80. Who do you know who can do this easily?

81. How is this like 'X' [*something your client has mentioned before*]?

82. What metaphor can you create that describes this task / capability?

83. Go forward to a time when you can do this easily. How did you learn it?

84. How will it feel to have mastered this?

85. What score from 1 – 10 would you give that describes your sense of your ability to do this?

86. What would it take to boost that score?

87. Which of your current resources will help you as you undertake this task?

Championing Your Client

This section is about holding your client in a safe space and acknowledging what is happening for them at this time. It can also take the form of a supportive statement that simply demonstrates understanding and takes the client forward before using a powerful question.

88. What new opportunities are opening up for you?

89. How does your life experience so far equip you for these new opportunities?

90. What is it about these opportunities that make them exciting?

91. How close are you to the end of the tunnel?

92. How are you going to use your power?

93. What are you like when you are at your best?

94. What do you really want to have happen here?

95. What do you need to start now?

96. What could you start now?

97. What is your uniqueness?

98. What makes you special?

99. You are in a dip, and that will change at some point.

100. Your performance on that occasion was not a true reflection of your potential.

101. You don't need to be held back by that, the next time will be different.

102. I understand that it doesn't feel like it right now, however you are going to come through this and perhaps even be more grateful for the experience.

103. This temporary slump is not who you are. You'll get through this valley and be on the next hill soon.

104. You're too capable to be held back by this for long.

105. You're so close to the finish line with this, just dig in and see it through.

106. It has been quite a climb; I know you're getting tired, but you're down to the last ten feet. You'll make it.

107. You know you are more than capable of rising above this.

108. What positive feedback would you give yourself?

109. How could you tap into that hidden wisdom at this moment?

110. What would the wise part of you recommend you do?

111. What does getting in touch with your intuition tell you?

112. As your champion, what would you want me to do?

113. How would you want me to be?

114. How could you do that for yourself?

Letting Go of Issues

These questions can enable an exploration of what it is that the client is holding onto that may not serve them so well. It also begins to explore what the 'cost' may be of having or not having certain behaviours / issues.

115. What do you think you need to let go of?

116. How have you tried to let go of this in the past?

117. What worked really well?

118. What would happen if you employed that tactic again?

119. What triggers worry you?

120. How clear are you about what you fear?

121. How else could you see this situation?

122. How would an alien who had just arrived on earth see this issue?

123. What would they make of it?

124. What makes your power and energy drain away?

125. How much of this drain is within your control?

126. What is the cost to you of playing it safe?

127. If you were not concerned about what anyone else thought, what would you do?

128. What have you not tried because you were concerned about looking good / pleasing others?

129. If it were completely safe, what would you risk?

130. How can you anchor a sense of safety as you take this step?

131. What would be the safe choice?

132. What would be the daring choice?

133. What do you fear might happen?

134. How would you cope with that?

135. What would it take for you to overcome your fears and take action?

136. What support do you want from me as your coach as you take this step?

137. When do you feel you are being productive rather than just active?

138. What will you do?

139. When will you do it?

140. What will it 'cost' to do it?

141. If there were no constraints what would you do?

142. If you suspended doubt what action would you take?

143. Are you happy with the way things are going?

144. If not, what are you going to do about it?

145. When will you do something about it?

146. What important choices are available to you now?

147. In five years' time what decision will you be glad you made now?

148. What is the most useful thing you could do right now to take you where you want to go?

149. What action will make the greatest difference?

150. What is your next step?

151. What changes do you need to initiate, and how will you initiate those changes?

152. What about the costs of changing – what are your plans to manage these?

153. Have you chosen the direction you are moving in?

154. What direction would you prefer?

155. What other choices do you have?

156. What are your options?

157. Which option best fits your goals?

158. By saying 'YES' to 'X', what are you saying 'NO' to?

159. How will you be fully alive this week?

160. What is it to live fully?

161. How would you 'live' out loud?

162. How will you be an artist in the world?

163. What do you notice about your recent direction?

164. How will you know this is the right direction?

165. What will you let go of to change course if needed?

166. In what direction are you moving now?

167. What is holding you back?

168. What is the cost of worry?

169. What quality of thought do you sacrifice?

170. When don't you trust how you will act?

171. What 'you' might show up?

172. What is the cost of not taking action?

173. What will enable you to move beyond your comfort zone?

174. How do you learn to trust movement?

175. When does movement turn into momentum?

176. How do you let go of your energy?

177. How can you be willing to have it so?

178. What chasm requires a big step?

179. What would that step be?

180. What different step could that be?

181. How will you know if things are going well?

182. What would you do now if you were already the person you're hoping to become?

183. What is missing for you?

184. What are you holding on to?

185. How can you / who can help you make that 'magic solution' become reality?

186. Where do you know you are stopping short?

187. What are you going to do now about that issue?

188. What are you tolerating in your work / home?

189. What do you put up with to avoid confrontation?

190. What do you tolerate to avoid conflict?

191. What do you tolerate to gain approval?

192. Who are you being nice to - possibly not yourself?

193. How long do you want to put up with them?

194. How will you eliminate unnecessary requests / actions?

195. If you start all over again from scratch, what would you do differently, knowing what you know now?

196. How can you manage yourself so that you can be yourself more of the time?

197. Does the issue really lie in the task, or the way you feel about the task?

198. What are you not holding on to, to gain approval?

Managing Your State

This section provides questions about your client's way of being or 'state'. States can vary enormously; different states can be more effective than others depending upon the situation. Identifying productive states is extremely useful in helping your client be fully resourceful.

199. What state do you have to be in to do this most effectively?

200. What state do you have to be to be available to learn?

201. What do you need to do to achieve that state?
202. What makes you feel stable and grounded?
203. What do you need to do to ensure you have more of this in your life?
204. Who can help you achieve this?
205. What makes you feel good?
206. Have you ever done anything really well, when you didn't feel confident?
207. What were the positive outcomes?
208. What do you notice about your energy levels?
209. What drains you?
210. How might you mitigate the loss of energy?
211. How does this impact on how you feel at different times of the day?
212. How are you being when you are at your most relaxed?
213. What do you notice?
214. How are you used to being as you go about your day?
215. On a scale of 1 – 10 how effective are you when you are being like this?
216. Who are you pretending to be?
217. What gives you the feel-good factor?
218. What reminds you of happy times?
219. How do you know when you are stressed?
220. What would be a simple strategy for changing your state when required?
221. What could you do that would ensure you have a resourceful state?
222. If you wanted to change your state; how would you do that?
223. Which way of being is most effective for you right now?

224. What can you learn from others who manage their state effectively?

Not Knowing

These questions work with uncertainty. Understanding how it impacts can assist your client to respond differently and utilise the benefits or minimize its draining capacity.

225. How much uncertainty are you living with right now?
226. How is this affecting you?
227. When was the last time you were in a situation like this?
228. What did you do?
229. What worked well?
230. What would you avoid in the future?
231. What might you have done differently?
232. What is it about this issue that makes it an issue?
233. What will it mean for your life / business / career if you don't 'X'?
234. What will be different about the way in which you see yourself if you do 'X'?
235. How does that fit in with your goal?
236. What is the worst thing / the best thing that could happen?
237. If you take this step, what would you do next?
238. What is the gift in this challenge?
239. What can you control in this situation?
240. How will it feel to do that?
241. What can't you control in the situation?
242. What might you control that you haven't been able to control?

243. How do you know?

244. What is it that you do know about yourself, that you would most like to be acknowledged for so far in your life?

245. If you were your own coach, what would you say to yourself right now?

246. What, in this situation, can you find to be grateful for?

247. What are you going to do differently tomorrow?

248. How would you summarise what you are going to do and by when?

249. Let us suppose you did know what the answer was, how would you know when you found it?

250. What would be different?

251. What is it that you don't know, that if you did know, would enable you to make the change easily and effortlessly right now?

252. If you did know, what would you do / say / feel / decide?

253. If I could give you the answer to what you want right now, what would the question be?

254. What is the greatest truth for you in this situation?

255. What is the truest thing you know about yourself in this situation?

256. What is missing, that if present, would have the biggest impact?

257. What do you really need to know?

258. How will knowing serve you?

259. And what will knowing that do for you?

260. What opportunity does not knowing present you?

261. Understanding there may be opportunities in uncertainty how does that change your view?

262. How could you confidently deal with uncertainty?

Recognising Self

> This section explores the client getting to know themselves and what some of their drivers are as they relate to operating within their world.

263. When you put yourself first, what would your decision be?
264. What do you want for yourself?
265. If you felt you could be totally selfish, what would you do?
266. What is 100% of what you want in this situation?
267. How could you get more of what will satisfy you?
268. How could you say no to this request?
269. Where do you want to draw boundaries with this?
270. What have you done recently that you should give yourself a pat on the back for?
271. What is your responsibility for what has been happening?
272. What early signs are there that things might be getting better / going all right?
273. When are you at your most resourceful?
274. What do you say to yourself about this issue?
275. What would it take for you to be your own strongest ally?
276. How will you hold on?
277. How will you know you're good enough?
278. What is the danger?
279. What is the opportunity?
280. How will you exploit that opportunity?
281. How will you use patience?
282. What is your leap in the dark?
283. How do you step open- hearted into the unknown?
284. How will you be bold?
285. What will you begin?

286. What is the cost of not taking action?
287. How will you find the courage to move beyond your comfort zone?
288. How do you protect yourself by not trying?
289. What would the first move be?
290. What 'auditions' do you skip because you believe you wouldn't get the part?
291. How do you give yourself acknowledgement?
292. What are you avoiding?
293. What are you unwilling to address?
294. What is the lie?
295. How aware are you of any repeating patterns?
296. When you think about this pattern, how does it serve you?
297. So, what is the bottom line / essence of this?
298. What gets in your way?
299. How might this limit what you get out of coaching?
300. Where else in life does this show up?
301. How is that working for you?
302. How is that serving you?
303. How important is your growth?
304. How much security are you willing to surrender?
305. What if 'why not' was the first question of every day?

My Favourite Questions

Chapter 5
Time Management

Contents:

Beliefs

> Beliefs are the principles / rules / assumptions that guide our actions, they are our reality and we act upon them. Questions that challenge them can cause change - moving the client forward into a different, more positive action or place.

1. What do you believe about time? [e.g. time is money, there is never enough time etc.]
2. How are these beliefs appropriate and in context with today?
3. What would you rather belief?
4. Did you believe the same things 10, 20 years ago?
5. So, what has changed in that time?
6. How is it still serving you?
7. What is really important to you about time?
8. How do you represent time in your mind?
9. What patterns do you notice in how you spend / use your time?
10. How does this reflect your desire to get things done?
11. How could you get everything done today and still have time for yourself?

12. How is this belief limiting your ability to manage time?

13. What would be more appropriate for you now?

14. Who are the key people you should be spending time with?

15. What are you putting off / avoiding?

16. How much time do you need?

17. What are you assuming about this situation?

18. What will you be doing in ten years' time?

19. What do you believe is getting in your way?

20. What do you believe is possible?

21. Where do you believe you can control time?

22. What do you have control over?

23. How much time would be enough?

24. What might you control that you haven't been able to in the past?

25. Where do you spent most of your time – past, present or future?

26. How in control of your time are you?

27. How will you use your control?

28. How controlling do you want to be?

29. What is your real work?

30. What will move it forward?

31. How much time are you focusing on 'busy' work?

32. How is focusing on that moving your real work forward?

33. What would happen if you turned your mobile / computer / telephone off for an hour / day / weekend?

34. What do you say to yourself at the end of the day?

35. What do you say to yourself at the start of each day?

36. Where could you find more time?

37. How do you 'waste' time?

Obstacles and Distractions

We have defined this section as being questions that relate to moving your client forward. Obstacles and distractions being something that prevent your client from moving forward and standing in their way.

38. How do you become distracted?

39. What did you notice that distracted you?

40. What happens to the other person when you become distracted?

41. What does that do for you?

42. Where might that lead you?

43. Where do you get caught up in trivialities?

44. How does that obstacle / distraction serve you as you understand it?

45. What do you want to try next instead?

46. What do you need to start or remove in order to have 'X'?

47. Taking 'action' tells you whether it is the right path or not, what do your actions tell you?

48. What is stopping you from achieving your goal?

49. Who could you delegate this task to?

50. What is stopping you from delegating it?

51. How much time could you free up if this task was delegated?

52. If this is a regular task – what other plan could you put in place?

53. How could you be more present?

54. What else are you thinking about?

55. What will be the immediate impact of this option without the distraction?

56. What will be the impact of this option in one year's time?
57. How are you avoiding spending time with 'X'?
58. What do you need to turn off?
59. What has stopped you sorting this out sooner?
60. Which phase are you in - planning or action?
61. How could you move it from planning to action?
62. So what needs to happen for 'X'?
63. And what else needs to happen for 'X'?
64. And what is the first thing that needs to happen?
65. What possibilities come to mind?
66. What more could you say about 'X'?
67. What might happen if you 'X'?
68. What are some of the specific things you have tried to move forward?
69. What does 'X' have to say about this?
70. When could you take a break from 'X'?
71. What would you have to do to ensure you could take that break?
72. How important to you, on a scale of 1 – 10, is it that you take that break?
73. When are you going to start it?
74. What will happen when the main distractions have vanished?
75. How could you get around this obstacle?
76. How good a distraction is that for you?
77. How are you putting things off?
78. How will waiting serve you?
79. How much energy are you spending avoiding this job?
80. If the obstacles are removed, how high will you climb?
81. What will you do differently to minimize your distractions?

Prioritising

This section focuses the client's attention on what and how they determine the order of dealing with the tasks they have at hand. It will enable them to think more clearly about how they utilise their time.

82. How is this the best use of your time?
83. How have you scheduled your time to satisfy your priorities?
84. Which are the key areas you would like / need to focus on?
85. How do you prioritise your time?
86. What is the most valuable use of your time right now?
87. What are the consequences of doing this?
88. What are the consequences of not doing this?
89. How could you apply the 80 / 20 rule here?
90. What would you love to do today?
91. What would bring you great joy in how you spend your time?
92. If you had been told you only had 6 months to live how would you choose to spend that time?
93. What would be important about those choices?
94. Who would you spend it with?
95. Where would you go?
96. How do you use your time?
97. How could you eliminate or reduce the time pressures that you experience?
98. When did how you vote to spend your time represent your values?
99. When have your vote and your values been in conflict?
100. How can you focus on the result, not the effort?

101. How balanced is your day / life / job?

102. Where is your attention / focus now?

103. Where would you like it to be?

104. Are you the only person who can do this?

105. Who would be the best person to take this on?

106. How will you know when the time is right for you?

107. How will you manage changes in your priorities?

108. Who needs to know that this is a priority for you?

109. When will you get it done by?

110. If 80% of your results come from 20% of your effort where should you be focusing your effort?

111. How can you make taking time out for relaxation, rejuvenation a priority?

112. What is it that you feel you should do?

113. What is it that you feel you must do?

114. What is it you feel you could do?

115. What is it that you feel you'd like to do?

116. What do you have to do?

117. What do you want to do?

118. What do you notice about the answers you have given to these questions?

119. How much of your work requires an immediate answer?

120. How do you prioritise - urgent or important matters first?

121. How does that work for you?

122. What would change if you reversed them?

123. Who determines the urgency / importance?

124. How much control do you have over determining urgency versus importance?

125. What would need to change to give you more control?

126. When you say you will 'try' what does that mean?

Pulling It All Together

> This section is to enable your client to take a small step back and see, hear and feel how they are using their time and how they could address their time issues.

127. Who do you think is excellent at time management?
128. How do they do it?
129. How might you instigate some of their practices?
130. What is a realistic assessment of the time it will take?
131. How important is it to you to get this done / finished?
132. What kind of timeline do you want to follow to get through this project?
133. So, when will you have had that done by?
134. How will you hold yourself accountable?
135. When will you know you have finished / achieved it?
136. How will you celebrate when you have achieved it?
137. How could you make this easy?
138. How can you incorporate free hours / days into your schedule?
139. How would you use that free hour / day?
140. How would having a free hour / day change you?
141. How do you balance time with yourself and time with others?
142. Time is an opportunity; how do you want to spend that resource?
143. How would you sum up how you had spent your day / week / month / year?
144. How creative have you been in your recent use of time?
145. How creative could you get?
146. What would that mean to you / your family / team?

147. How could you get totally up to date now?

148. What works for you?

149. How could you do more of that?

150. What effect could that have on your use of time?

151. What action would you like to take away and implement today?

Saying 'YES and 'NO'

Saying 'YES' and 'NO' explores how your client is voting with the way they manage themselves and how they spend their time. It is a section that can highlight discrepancies, especially when utilising a balance wheel exercise.

152. What do you want to say 'YES' to in your life?

153. What do you want to say 'NO' to in your life?

154. What did you notice when you had finished completing the balance wheel?

155. What strikes you now when you think about the wheel?

156. What more is there about the balance in your wheel?

157. What will you do now and say 'NO' to in order to do the 'YES' things

158. How do your choices about how you spend time reflect your highest values?

159. What have you learned about yourself with regard to spending time?

160. How often do you find yourself rushing around because you said 'YES'?

161. What is the cost of that behaviour?

162. How much time do you have left (1 yr = 8,760 hours)?

163. How do you want to spend it?

164. What is the 'YES' and 'NO' of this choice?

165. How will you vote with the choices available?

166. What one thing could you do (that you are not doing now) that if you did on a regular basis would make a tremendous positive difference to your personal / working life?

167. How is what you are choosing to do going to get you closer to achieving your goals / objectives?

168. What are you actually saying 'YES' to?

169. What are you actually saying 'NO' to?

170. How does that honour your highest values?

171. What is the worst that could happen by saying 'NO'/'YES'?

172. What would you like to happen?

173. What could you do to manage this?

174. What are you inventing to avoid the important things?

175. Where do you need to make clear requests?

176. What would it take to move you toward 'YES'?

177. By doing 'X', you are accepting 'Y' - is this by choice?

178. What limits are needed around your work / life to ensure you have enough time for 'X'?

179. If you are not going to do 'X', what are you going to do?

180. How do you want to define how much time you are going to spend on 'X'?

181. How often do you want to spend time looking at 'X'?

182. How much time will you spend generating balance?

183. What things will you now change because you can say 'YES' or 'NO'?

184. What impact is making clear, conscious 'YES' and 'NO' decisions making in your life?

185. What opportunities could you say 'YES' to?

Vision and Purpose

Questions that enable the client to articulate an inspiring future. They also enable clients to relate the managing of their time to that future, their purpose and to being their most effective and efficient self.

186. What would an inspiring future contain?
187. What values are being expressed in this future?
188. What action would be aligned with your vision?
189. What is really important as you make this choice?
190. How does getting caught up in trivialities keep you from fulfilling your vision and purpose?
191. Where are you trapped in action?
192. Looking from an elevated view, what is significant about the choice you're making towards your future?
193. What is the central issue here?
194. How does it relate to who you are?
195. What will be the consequences of not paying attention to what you really want / matters to you?
196. Will this matter 5 to 10 years from now – what could you do that will?
197. What do you want to achieve?
198. How do you want to achieve it?
199. How is what you are doing moving you towards that goal / objective?
200. How does the vision / dream of yourself fit with reality?
201. What / where is the difference?
202. What needs to change to make it a reality?
203. What happens when you imagine 'X'?
204. What options have you considered with regard to time?

205. What options have you not yet considered?

206. What limitations might you be placing on this?

207. How else could you think about this?

208. What is useful about this?

209. How successful do you want to be in the way you manage time?

210. How will you / your team / organisation be viewed by your peers/industry?

211. If you were to create a powerful vision of where you want to be in 5 / 10 years' time how would you describe it?

212. How would you describe it to your team / family / organisation?

213. How does that vision fit with how you currently spend your time?

214. How does that vision fit with your purpose?

215. If you were to create a metaphor for how you currently spend your time what would that be?

216. If you were to create a metaphor for how you would rather be spending your time what would that be?

217. What do you notice about the difference between these two metaphors?

218. Which one appeals most to you?

219. What appeals most about it?

220. How could you incorporate it into your vision of where you want to be?

221. What drives your use of your time?

222. If you could change one thing to free up more time what would that be?

223. A vision brings clarity and focus – how clear and focused is yours?

224. What needs changing?

225. What could be acting as a smokescreen for you?

226. What would be a more effective use of your time in realising your vision?

227. If you were to create a vision board – what would be on it?

Chapter 6
Influencing

Contents:

Awareness

> Awareness is all about encouraging curiosity and noticing; enabling the client to make discoveries that can increase their knowledge. Understanding more about ourselves and others is a good start for improving influencing skills.

1.   What do we really need to talk about?
2.   Where do your boundaries lie?
3.   How receptive are you to hearing a hard truth?
4.   I'd like to explore 'X', what would stop that from being okay?
5.   How receptive are you to others commenting on your behaviour?
6.   What would you not like to hear that you know is true?
7.   What would enable us to go further with this issue?
8.   What would happen if we devoted more time to 'X'?
9.   How slowly do you wish to proceed with this issue?
10. What is the underlying pattern that you have observed?
11. What do others see?
12. How do you know what they see?
13. Can we go there in more detail?

14. What do you mean by 'X'

15. And what does 'X' mean for you?

16. What is the benefit of the present situation?

17. What are the disadvantages of the present situation?

18. What are you contributing to this situation?

19. What would be the most powerful question I could ask you right now?

20. What question would open up a different possibility?

21. What question could you ask yourself right now?

22. How will confusion serve you?

23. How will 'X' affect the wider systems you belong to?

24. How do you stop yourself?

25. What would that give you that you wouldn't otherwise have?

26. What do you expect of yourself?

Business Development

Business development is all about the activity of pursuing strategic opportunities and understanding requirements. These questions challenge your client to explore, delve deeper and then take action.

27. What prompted you/ your company to look into this?

28. What are your expectations/ requirements for this product/ service?

29. What process did you go through to determine your needs?

30. How do you see this happening?

31. What is it that you'd like to see accomplished?

32. With whom have you had success in the past?

33. With whom have you had difficulties in the past?

34. Can you help me understand that a little better?

35. What does that mean?

36. How does that process work now?

37. What challenges does that process create?

38. What challenges has that created in the past?

39. What are the best things about that process?

40. What other items should we discuss?

41. What do you see as the next action steps?

42. What is your timeline for implementing/ purchasing this type of service/ product?

43. What other data points should we know before moving forward?

44. What budget has been established for this?

45. What are your thoughts?

46. Who else is involved in this decision?

47. What could make this no longer a priority?

48. What is changed since we last talked?

49. What concerns do you have?

50. How did you get involved in...?

51. What kind of challenges are you facing?

52. What is the most important priority to you with this? Why?

53. What other issues are important to you?

54. What would you like to see improved?

55. How do you measure that?

56. What prompted you/ your company to look into this?

57. What are your expectations/ requirements for this product/ service?

58. What process did you go through to determine your needs?

59. How do you see this happening?

60. What is it that you'd like to see accomplished?

61. With whom have you had success in the past?

62. With whom have you had difficulties in the past?

63. Can you help me understand that a little better?

64. What does that mean?

65. Which USP fits best with your company values?

66. How could you align the benefits of this product / service to fit your client's company values?

67. What qualities do you think your client sees in you?

68. What other items should we discuss?

69. What do you see as the next action steps?

70. What is your timeline for implementing/ purchasing this type of service/ product?

71. What other data points should we know before moving forward?

72. What budget has been established for this?

73. What are your thoughts?

74. Who else is involved in this decision?

75. What could make this no longer a priority?

76. What is changed since we last talked?

77. What concerns do you have?

78. How did you get involved in 'X'?

79. What kind of challenges are you facing?

80. What is the most important priority to you with this? Why?

81. What other issues are important to you?

82. What would you like to see improved?

83. How do you measure that?

84. Where can you serve your client/customer best?

85. How can you serve your client/customer best?

86. Where are you an automatic 'NO' or 'YES'?

87. What are you tolerating that is sapping your energy?

88. What space can you create? [Nature abhors a vacuum]

89. How can I help you make an easy decision?

90. What do you hope to gain from this meeting?

91. What are the key messages you/your client is wanting to get across?

92. What are the benefits of what you/your client is offering?

93. What are you really selling here?

94. How do you feel about 'selling' yourself?

95. How much of your customer base comes through referrals?

96. How would I know if someone would be a good referral client for your business?

97. Is there anyone else in your organisation, or that you know, who would benefit from your services?

98. What do you see as the USP (Unique Selling Point) of the product/service you are offering?

99. What does your client/customer see as the USP of the product/service?

100. What are the alternative USPs of the product/service?

101. What is important to you when you are deciding on a product/service?

102. How could you develop further empathy with your client/customer to develop understanding of the product/service?

103. What would that give you that you wouldn't otherwise have?

104. What do you expect of yourself?

105. How did you make a decision before?

106. Where do we go from here?

Change Management

This section is all about the discipline that guides how you problem solve and prepare, equip and support successful adoptions of change to drive yourself and your organisation successfully forward. These questions explore that area.

107. What is the problem you are trying to solve?
108. How do you know it is a problem?
109. How do you know that is really the problem?
110. Where is it a problem?
111. Why is it a problem?
112. When is it a problem?
113. Who is it a problem for?
114. What is the root cause of the problem?
115. How will you know the problem is solved?
116. What is the simplest solution to the problem?
117. If the problem was solved what would that give you?
118. Where are you going?
119. What is your goal?
120. What else would be solved if this problem was solved?
121. Where are you starting from?
122. How will you know when you've arrived at your desired destination?
123. How will you get there?
124. Who do you know that has taken this path before?
125. Whose help do you need?
126. What is your plan?
127. How will you know if you're winning or losing?
128. What is the change you are seeking to make?
129. What will be different when the change is achieved?

130. Who are the key stakeholders you need to get on board?

131. How will you influence them to support you?

132. What do your stakeholders need from you?

133. Who is impacted by what you want to do?

134. How ready are they for the change?

135. What will you need to do to assist them to be ready?

136. How can you help them engage with your change?

137. What will success look like, feel like?

138. If you imagine you have been successful in achieving what you want, what steps did it take to get there?

139. What was the first step?

140. What are the key milestones to achieve your plan?

141. How will you monitor your milestone deliverables?

142. What dependencies do you have?

143. What assumptions are you making?

144. What risks are possible?

145. How will you mitigate the risks?

146. What are you willing to change?

Modeling

These questions can lead your client to improve performance by recreating the excellence seen in others or themselves in other areas of their life.

147. Who are you modeling?

148. What makes them the best?

149. When have you ever done anything like this?

150. What skills did you employ?

151. What would you carry forward to this new situation?

152. Who do you know who can do this easily?

153. How is this situation like 'X' [naming something the client has done before]?
154. Step forward to a time when you can do it easily – how did you do it?
155. What did you do to learn it?
156. How will it feel to have mastered this?
157. Give a score 1 – 10 that describes your sense of ability to do this – what would it take to boost it by 2 / 3 / 4 points?
158. What resources will help you undertake this?
159. What is your sticking point?
160. When do you engage in the activity / behavior you want to model?
161. Where do you engage in the activity / behavior you want to model?
162. What do you do when you are in those times and places?
163. What is important to you when you are doing those activities / behaviours?
164. Who are you being when you are engaged in those activities / behaviours?
165. Who else are you serving when you undertake those activities / behaviours?
166. What is different about what you did then and there from what you are doing here and now?
167. What do you need to change to enable you to role model those activities / behaviours?
168. How long will it take for you to develop those behaviours you want to model?
169. How are the pieces going to fit together?
170. What questions would you like to ask, to gain insights from your role model?

171. What could they teach you?

172. If you were to have a conversation with the younger / older you – what would you ask them?

173. What would enable you to believe you can be as proficient as your role models?

174. What steps do you need to take on your journey to proficiency?

175. When you are in this type of situation what are the goals and objectives, which guide your actions?

176. What do you usually use as evidence to know you are accomplishing your goals?

177. What specifically are the steps and activities you use?

178. When you experience unexpected problems or difficulties in achieving those goals what specific actions or activities do you take?

179. What made this possible?

180. What made this happen?

181. What would enable you to practice more often?

182. How has this worked for you before?

Motivation

Motivation is the driving force by which we work towards our goals. It's an essential component that is required in order for us to take action and stay on course to achievement. These questions explore the client's motivation.

183. Where have you experienced your greatest motivation?

184. What was present?

185. How can you experience that again?

186. What are the five things that you value most in your life?

187. What are the three most important goals in your life?

188. What interference could prevent them from happening?

189. What could happen if you were really successful?

190. What would you do if you won a substantial amount of money?

191. What would you do if you had no physical or mental limitations?

192. If you knew you had a limited time left, what would you change?

193. What have you always wanted to do, and been afraid to attempt?

194. Reflecting on the things you have done, what made you feel most important?

195. What gave you the greatest joy?

196. What gave you the greatest satisfaction?

197. What gave you the greatest energy after you'd done it?

198. What is the major purpose in your life?

199. What are your top three strengths?

200. What are your three most prevalent weaknesses / areas of development?

201. If you could be granted one skill or ability, what would it be?

202. What gives you the greatest pleasure and satisfaction in your life?

203. What legacy would you like to leave?

204. What three things have you been putting off?

205. What items in your life, that you currently have would you eliminate?

206. Who is living the life you admire?

207. Can you describe what you think it is like to live that life.

208. What is the kind of work you wish to be doing?

209. What will you do to move you towards that kind of work?

210. What will you be most proud of when you are much older?

211. What are the three things that changed in the world because you lived?

212. What would you attempt if you knew you could not fail?

213. What would the consequences for others be?

214. What would you want if you knew you didn't have to be unhappy about not getting it?

215. What will the 'corridor' chat be about you after you've gone?

216. What would you like people to say about you?

217. What would you do with your money if you had all you could ever need?

218. How would you live your life if you knew you were going to be gone in five years' time?

219. What would you feel you've missed if you only had 24 hours to live?

220. What can you do about that now?

221. What are the four or five things you are most glad that you did?

222. What will absolutely motivate you to 'X' and how will you feel once you have?

223. What needs to happen for 'X'?

224. What will your life be like when you are able to 'X'?

225. Who already does this really well?

226. How did they crack this problem when they had it?

227. What would you rather have?

228. What will be different if you had this?

229. When will you be ready to go and get what you want?

Personal Impact/Visibility

> Relates to the impact a client has on themselves and others around them. How they might be seen, heard and felt in their environment.

230. What values are being expressed when you do this?
231. What action would be aligned with your vision?
232. What is really important as you make this choice?
233. Where do you get caught in trivialities?
234. What do your actions tell me about you?
235. Where are you trapped in action?
236. Where do you trap others?
237. When you stand back and look at this, what is significant about your choices?
238. What is the central issue here?
239. How does it relate to who you are?
240. How does it relate to those around you?
241. What will be the consequences of not paying attention to what you really want / matters to you?
242. Will this matter 5 to 10 years from now?
243. What could you do that will?
244. When was the last time you made an impact?
245. What did you do that worked well – what were you doing, saying, thinking, and feeling?
246. What will remind you of this time?
247. What were the key learnings from this time?
248. What would you most like to impart to others?
249. How will you go about sharing your skills?
250. What would enable you to be clear on the needs and desired outcomes of the others involved?

251. Who do you know that regularly makes an impact?
252. What can you learn from them?
253. What would you need to do to put some of that into practice?
254. What will you need to do to get into the best possible frame of mind for this?
255. What preparatory exercises / rituals work for you?
256. How will you position yourself to have the most impact?
257. How will you physically position yourself for the most impact?
258. What do you know about the preferred styles of the others involved?
259. What do you need to do to accommodate others?
260. What is it about your style that works?
261. How can you vary your language / approach to match this style?
262. How will you acknowledge their needs / perspective?
263. What impact can you demonstrate without words?
264. How can you engage with the others involved?
265. What can you say to encourage yourself?
266. How do you visualise yourself making an impact?
267. What will you be doing?
268. What will it be like when you've achieved your outcome?
269. How will you know that what you're doing is working?
270. What changes could you make to your approach?
271. How will you remain centred / grounded / present?
272. What is the biggest impact you will make by just being yourself?
273. Who has had a great influence on your business/life?
274. What was it that they did that caused such an influence?

275. What was it that you took away from that situation?

276. Whose list are you on for being influential in their lives?

277. Who do you want to be in this situation?

278. How is this really impacting you?

279. How is this really impacting your work?

280. How is this really impacting your relationships?

281. What is your mission with this?

282. How is this reflected in how you present yourself?

283. What commercial or social impact do you have?

284. What signals are you putting out – to your team, boss, partner etc.?

285. How are you delivering against your promises?

286. How do you currently signal your trustworthiness?

287. What signals do you like your team to give you?

288. What is your 'brand'?

289. How are you promoting this in what you do and say?

290. What do you need to do to increase your visibility?

291. How visible do you believe you are right now?

292. Who says you are not visible?

293. What is it that they do notice?

294. How do you know you are being recognised?

295. What needs to happen for you to know you're being recognised?

296. What do you do to recognise others?

297. What did you teach others?

298. How did you know you had made a positive impact?

299. How did that make you feel?

300. How could you do more of it?

301. Is your impact through 'doing' or 'being'?

302. Which feels more comfortable to you?

Rapport Building

Rapport is something to continually work on; it enables mutual respect and trust to build within relationships. For the client, it is all about noticing and understanding the different worlds that others operate in and endeavouring to be in their shoes where they can.

303. How would you describe your rapport with others?
304. When is it easy to relate with others?
305. How do you relate to yourself?
306. What kind of relationship do you have with yourself?
307. In which environments do you feel most comfortable / uncomfortable?
308. What makes you feel most alive and alert?
309. Who do you know who you trust / respect?
310. What is it about them that enables you to trust / respect them?
311. Who do you know who is a good listener?
312. What makes them a good listener?
313. When was the last time you felt really listened to?
314. How do you listen?
315. What do you notice when you are listening to someone?
316. If someone was to give you feedback on how well you listen how would they mark you on a scale of 1 – 10?
317. How do you know when the message you are giving has been received?
318. How do you prefer to take information in?
319. How do you establish rapport with people who are totally different from you?
320. What are the unwritten 'rules' of the team / organisation?

321. What would you say is your communication style?
322. How is it working for you?
323. What could you change to become even more effective?
324. What is your understanding of the corporate culture?
325. How closely are you aligned with that culture?
326. How could you disagree with 'X' and still maintain a good relationship with them?
327. What is a really resourceful state for you?
328. How can you create that resourceful state in real time?
329. What do you do to maintain consistency in your relationships?
330. What would you do differently if you were on the receiving end of that conversation / action?
331. What could you do to mitigate negatives reactions?
332. What triggers that negative reaction?
333. What differences do you notice when you are relating to different people?
334. What is it like for you when you focus totally on one person?
335. How do you hold your body when you are totally focused on the other person?
336. What do you observe of yourself when communicating with people you find difficult?
337. What is it that others do who appear to have good rapport with most people?
338. How do you become disengaged with someone?
339. What happens to the other person when you become disengaged?
340. What do you notice about your own body language?
341. If you changed it what would happen?

Stakeholder Management

> Stakeholders are all those who can affect or be affected by the actions of your client.

342. How large is your circle of influence?

343. What would increase it?

344. How would you do that?

345. Who are your main stakeholders?

346. Putting yourself in their shoes, what do you think their priorities are?

347. What would enable you to know that for sure?

348. What do you think motivates them in this situation?

349. Which stakeholders do you spend most time on?

350. How are you currently communicating with them?

351. On whom do you think you should spend more time?

352. With which stakeholders do you need to spend more time?

353. With which stakeholders do you need / want to communicate more?

354. What is the underlying message you want to get across?

355. How could you alter the way you communicate it?

356. What are the objectives of each of the stakeholders?

357. How do those align with your objectives?

358. How can you work together to meet your objectives?

359. How are you relating to your stakeholders?

360. What is it about your objectives that are similar?

361. How are they different?

362. What would happen if you were to create a strategic alliance with them?

363. What can you learn from them?

364. What do you need to stop doing?

365. What do you need to start doing?
366. What sort of information would you like to share with your stakeholders?
367. How could you become more flexible in your dealings?
368. What do you notice about the situation you are in?
369. What do you notice about the situation looking at it from their perspective?
370. What constraints or challenges do you think they may be facing?
371. What can you do differently to ensure a successful relationship?

Chapter 7
Leadership

Contents:

Beliefs

> Beliefs are the principles / rules / assumptions that guide our actions, they are our reality and we act upon them. Questions that challenge them can enable reflection and cause change; moving the client forward into a different, more positive action.

1. Does this situation echo a former situation from the past?

2. How did you show up today?

3. How are you showing up right now?

4. What rules are you currently running for yourself?

5. What have you not noticed that is important?

6. Who believes in you?

7. What do you believe about yourself?

8. Who do you want to believe in you and why?

9. How do you like to be managed?

10. How does this fit with your personal values?

11. What are some of the best moments you've had in your company / career?

12. What are you like when you are at your best?

13. What do you value most about your work?

14. How would you describe leadership?

15. How much is enough / good enough?

16. How often is enough?

17. If you weren't here for a month, what wouldn't get done?

18. Which is more important to you - to be right or to be respected?

19. Which is more important to you - to be liked or viewed as efficient?

20. What is more important to you - to be understood or be understanding?

21. What are your beliefs / rules around this issue?

22. Which are helpful?

23. Which are unhelpful?

24. In what ways do you want to be different?

25. If you have difficulty delegating, what possible explanation is there for this?

26. What do you do that you can no longer afford to do in the same way?

27. Who do you know who displays the skills you wish to acquire?

28. What is it that they do differently?

29. What could you learn about their style?

30. What steps could you begin to take that would enable you to practice what you see / feel / hear?

31. What is your unique contribution?

32. How could you be more by doing less?

Conflict

This section explores where differences occur. The client can explore the root causes, nature and solutions to resolution.

33. Where do you know you are in conflict?
34. When is conflict more important than compromise?
35. When do you compromise?
36. When is compromise appropriate?
37. When is compromise incongruent, out of alignment with who you are and what you cherish?
38. What is the fear or danger in compromise?
39. How will you hold on to what is important to you?
40. What is the opportunity in this conflict?
41. What are the emotions you are trying to avoid here?
42. What do you seek to avoid?
43. What would the other party notice about you in a conflict situation?
44. What do you notice about your part in this?
45. What do you resent most about 'X'?
46. What do you think you might be doing that would cause other people to fear / mistrust / resent you?
47. What unintended messages might you be sending in this situation?
48. What would a fly on the wall say was going on?
49. What would the other party see you doing?
50. What would you have liked the other person to say?
51. What do you think the other person would have liked you to say or do?
52. Why do you think they didn't?
53. Why didn't you?

54. What would you like to have said?

55. What stopped you saying it?

56. What would your best self say or do here?

57. What is stopping you from facing up to this?

58. What is the consequence of not doing that?

59. What is the danger here?

60. What is the real issue for you in all this?

61. To what extent do you think your perceptions and expectations of 'X' may be contributing to the problems in your relationship with them?

62. How sure are you that the other person knows your intentions?

63. What indicators do you have to know you have been heard?

64. Who do you know who handles this in a different way?

65. What do they do?

66. If the worst happened what would be the silver lining?

67. When do you choose to be hurt by a conflict?

68. What could you do that would enable you to step back?

69. How would you deal with it if you were a man / woman / customer / CEO etc.?

70. If this issue were an animal / car how would you describe it?

71. How could this image assist your path to resolution?

72. What can you do to create / maintain harmony?

73. Where do the boundaries lie for you between the company and you as an individual?

74. What triggers an escalation for you?

75. How could you distract yourself at that moment?

76. What change would that bring about?

Decision-making

Questions which explore the client's strategies for decision making and being an effective leader.

77. What do you consider when making a decision?

78. How does this differ if it is unpopular?

79. How do your values align with your decision making?

80. What is the most important decision you are facing?

81. What is keeping you from making it?

82. What decisions did you avoid this week?

83. When will you have the courage to tackle this issue / pursue this course of action?

84. What will sustain you as you make this potentially unpopular decision?

85. How will you feel about this decision when you look back at it in two years time?

86. What does your gut instinct tell you?

87. What else could you do?

88. What else have you done?

89. What were the differences between the best and worst (career) decisions you have made?

90. What would be the best way for you to convey the pros and cons when making a decision?

91. Who else exerts control over your decisions?

92. What will you do for them to support your decision?

93. What would have to change for you to rule in solutions you have ruled out?

94. What is the real decision your trying to make?

95. What could you do that was neither 'X' nor 'Y'?

96. What is the most outrageous solution to this?

97. What is the boldest thing you could do?

98. What is the riskiest thing you could do?

99. What is stopping you from going ahead?

100. How could you make that become a calculated risk?

101. What is the issue that requires a speedy decision?

102. What specifications does the decision need to satisfy?

103. What solution will satisfy those specifications?

104. What action will be required to follow through on your decision?

105. What kind of feedback will let you know if this decision is appropriate?

106. If you did know the answer what would it be?

107. What would you do if your bonus / life / job depended on the satisfactory resolution of this issue?

108. Who else can support you in this issue?

Feedback

> Giving and receiving information that feeds the client forward into performance improvements. Learning is always possible in the feedback (see page 40 too).

109. How open to feedback are you?

110. What could you do to improve your openness to feedback?

111. How much might you have contributed to the problem?

112. What reaction do you have to your mistakes?

113. What reaction do you have to the mistakes of others?

114. What would the options be if you could look at this from a different view?

115. When do you most appreciate feedback?

116. When do you least appreciate feedback?

117. How do you most appreciate feedback being given to you?

118. How would your colleagues be able to tell if our coaching has been successful?

119. What will you do to make it possible to hear challenging feedback messages?

120. If your direct reports could really say what they think, without fear of offending, what might they tell you?

121. What could you do to obtain timelier, more constructive feedback?

122. What could help you become more fully receptive to challenging feedback?

123. What impression do people have of you?

124. What do you think you might be doing that might reinforce other people's impression of you?

125. What positive and constructive feedback would you give yourself?

126. What is your most effective way of giving feedback?

127. How do you maintain rapport with difficult message delivery?

128. What would make your feedback more effective?

Note to coach: a great acronym for giving feedback[2]

129. S - in what **S**ITUATION did this occur?

130. A - what **A**CTIVITY was observed and by whom?

131. I - what **I**MPACT did this activity have?

132. L - what did it **L**EAD to / or what was the **L**EARNING from it?

---

[2] *Feedback Model – S.A.I.L, courtesy of Jan Elfline (1998)*

Managing Others

This section allows your client to explore and develop their personal effectiveness in individual and team management.

133. What would your colleagues / staff not want to tell you?
134. What did you do today that helped your direct reports / colleagues perform?
135. What did you do today that got in the way of their performance?
136. What could you have done to enhance their performance?
137. What makes you avoid the conversation with 'X'?
138. What feelings do you have about it?
139. Where is that feeling coming from?
140. How might that emotion affect whether you achieve the outcome you want?
141. What do you need to control about this situation?
142. Why might you need to control?
143. How do you impact the team?
144. How could you find the courage to do what you think is right?
145. How could you have done this differently/better?
146. What do you think you do to enhance and empower?
147. How do you acknowledge good work with your staff / others?
148. What would happen if your employees were very motivated?
149. How much do you respect your colleagues?
150. How do you know they respect you?
151. How would 'X' handle this?
152. What do you / could you do to show that you care?

153. What does this mean for you?

154. What permissions have you given others?

155. What permissions have you given yourself?

156. When do you get the best out of others?

157. What is needed to do to enhance your team relationships?

158. What improvements could you make today?

159. What would change today if you made these improvements?

160. How would I know they are happening?

161. Who are your strongest members of staff?

162. How do they generate that strength?

163. What will you do to ensure the development of all team members?

164. What is it that they do that makes them have this quality?

165. What are you doing to ensure that they're happy and motivated?

166. Who are your weakest members of staff?

167. What makes you notice them?

168. What is your plan for the weaker members of staff?

169. How can you change your perception of them?

Managing Self – Limits and Fears

Clients can identify self-limiting ways of thinking and behaving, thus enabling them to create new, more effective strategies.

170. If you were the person you really want to be, how would you approach this situation?

171. What anxieties can you identify about achieving your goal of 'X'? [promotion, transfer etc.]

172. How would you surface these?
173. What clear messages are you sending?
174. Where might your messages lack clarity?
175. How does fear of criticism affect your actions?
176. What positive feedback would you give yourself?
177. How can you manage your sensitivity to criticism so that you can be yourself more of the time?
178. What is the question you wouldn't like someone to ask you about your work?
179. What is the question you wouldn't like to be asked right now?
180. Where are you most comfortable?
181. What permission have you given yourself?
182. Who do you need to give you permission to do this?
183. What is stopping you from giving yourself permission?
184. What are you noticing / choosing not to notice?
185. What are you growing out of?
186. What do you need to let go of?
187. What do you think you should be growing out of?
188. What steps will you take to do so?
189. What do you say to yourself silently, that you could say out loud now?
190. Who is your harshest critic?
191. Who are you in danger of growing into?
192. Who is the person you want to avoid becoming like?
193. What can you do now to prevent that from happening?
194. What could you do without permission that would show what you are capable of?
195. What habit(s) do you have, which you would like to change / get rid of?

196. What is the first step to breaking this habit?
197. What habit could you develop, which would support your goals?
198. How could you substitute one for the other?
199. What has to shift in your thinking about this?
200. What would be a clearer way of saying that?
201. What would positively stretch you now?
202. What would your worst enemy say about you?
203. Who would / could they be saying this to?
204. What will enable that view to change?
205. What would change if they saw a different you?
206. How / when do you give yourself permission to dream?
207. What would happen if you did more than just dream?

Managing Self – Self-awareness

Questions to discover the degree to which clients can honestly explore themselves.

208. How far can you go in your own thinking?
209. What is the biggest lie you have told yourself recently?
210. What did it achieve?
211. What don't you know that you don't know?
212. What didn't you know that you don't know?
213. What don't you know that you do know?
214. What is it about you that made you notice that behaviour in someone else?
215. What is your best (most useful) mistake recently?
216. Who are you trying to please?
217. What insights would you like to bring to our session?
218. How important to you is it to like yourself?

219. Who do you need to like you?
220. Will knowing this make you like yourself more or less?
221. What could you do today that would make you like yourself more?
222. Where are you most confident?
223. What do others see?
224. How do you demonstrate your capabilities?
225. How will coaching make your best better?
226. What could you do more of that would raise your presence?
227. What do you need to drive your own effectiveness?
228. How much do you respect yourself?
229. How would you explain this to your children / partner / family?
230. How / what do you feel?
231. What are your responsibilities here?
232. What does this situation / experience tell you about yourself?
233. What kind of role model do you think you represent here?
234. What kind do you want to represent?
235. What need are you addressing when you behave in this way?
236. What would you ask yourself if you were me?
237. If you were to look back at yourself from the future, what could you have learned from it?
238. Who are you?
239. Who do you want to be?
240. With whom do you compare yourself?
241. With whom would you like to be compared?
242. Why that person?

243. Who is in control of this situation?

244. Who knows who is in control?

245. Who can change things?

246. Who will implement that change?

247. Who owns your time?

248. Whose opinion do you value?

249. What are you like at your best?

250. How would your staff / boss describe you as being at your best?

251. What do you notice now that you were unaware of before?

252. If you looked in the mirror now, what would you observe about yourself?

253. What would help you become more aware?

254. What do you know about yourself?

255. What do you not know about yourself?

256. How do you acknowledge yourself?

257. How do you stay in the present?

258. What would change if you do?

259. What are you valued for?

260. What do you value yourself for?

261. What captures the essence of you?

262. How could you summarise this into something truly memorable?

263. What happens if you turn up the volume on that statement about yourself – how does it sound?

264. Is there anything that other (key) people don't understand about you?

265. How will you share this with them?

266. How does the normal 'you' differ from the 'you' under stress?

267. What pulls you back from this stress?

268. How do you make sure you are honest with yourself?

269. What have you done so far to improve things?

270. What isn't working well at the moment?

271. What is working well at the moment?

272. What have you identified that you did exceptionally well before?

273. What are you prepared to do differently now?

274. What enabled you to be in charge of your own destiny in the past?

275. How did you judge your success in the past?

276. What would be worth re-creating?

277. How does your story differ from X's?

278. What useful insights can you infer from that?

279. In what ways are you indispensable?

280. What could you / do you want to do to change that?

281. Do you know that or believe it?

282. What would you best friends say about you?

Motivation

Motivation is the driving force by which we work towards our goals. It is an essential component that is required in order for us to take action and stay on course to achievement. These questions explore the client's motivation as a leader.

283. What energises you?

284. How much worse does it have to get before you choose to do something different?

285. On a scale of 1 – 10 - how courageous do you feel?

286. What are the three things you have to be really good at?

287. Which do you feel least confident about?

288. How ready are you for change?

289. What do you care about?

290. What makes you care?

291. How could you reward yourself?

292. How much [*money, time, recognition etc.*] do you need to be happy?

293. How will you increase these?

294. When is enough, enough?

295. What are you addicted to?

296. How easily do you get bored?

297. What bores you?

298. What do you do to stop the boredom?

299. What is your contract with yourself?

300. Will this make you feel better or worse about yourself?

301. How will it take you nearer to where you want to go?

302. What is most important to you?

303. What would you need to do to make this job more meaningful / inspirational / stretching?

304. How fulfilled are you on a scale of 1 – 10?

305. When you think of your ideal position, how does what you're doing now differ?

306. How could you begin to fill the gap between where you are now and where you want to be?

307. Who do you admire most at work – what is it about them?

308. What would your manager / leader need to do to get the very best from you?

309. How will you inform them?

310. When you think about your current or next role, what are the things you would most like to do?

311. What did you 'get' from your last important role?

312. What would enable you to move forward?

313. What would you need to have in order to progress towards successful delivery of your most pressing tasks?

314. How committed are you to taking affirmative action to change things?

315. What would the best leader in your company do?

316. What would you do now if you were already the person you're hoping to become?

317. What will it mean for your life / career if you don't do it?

318. How much of your work is enjoyably challenging?

319. How can you increase the enjoyment?

320. How pure are your intentions?

321. If this is what you want to do, why haven't you started?

322. If you were independently wealthy, what would make you still come to work?

323. What is it that your work gives you above money?

324. Could you get that any other way?

325. What could increase your commitment?

326. What do you fear most?

327. What do you want people to say about you after you have gone?

328. What do you want to be remembered for?

329. What makes you feel valued?

330. What makes you get out of bed in the morning?

331. What makes you think you'd rather stay there?

332. What messages do you want to hear / give?

333. What stops you from walking away?

334. What three things would make a difference to how you feel, if you simply focused on doing them?

335. Where is the enjoyment in what you do?

336. What really matters to you?

337. If you were coaching yourself right now, what would you focus on?

338. What is it about this topic that makes it important to you right now?

339. You know what you need to do, but what do you choose?

340. Which of your values is driving your motivation with this?

341. Where / who do you go to for your inspiration?

Obstacles

We have defined this section as being questions that relate to moving your client forward. Obstacles in Leadership being things that prevent your client from moving forward and that stand in their way.

342. What is getting in your way?

343. What area under your responsibility are you most satisfied with?

344. What area under your responsibility are you least satisfied with?

345. What part of your responsibilities are you avoiding right now?

346. What chasm requires a big leap?

347. What would that leap be?

348. What could you do today?

349. What is the hesitation about getting started?

350. What baggage might you be bringing to this conversation?

351. What are the major challenges you're facing right now?

352. What are you doing to address these?

353. What are you achieving in these challenges right now?

354. What is holding you back?

355. What obstacles hold you back in your position?

356. If all obstacles disappeared, what would you do?

357. What is your greatest fear?

358. Where do you feel most stuck?

359. What happens just before you get stuck?

360. Where are the walls of your box?

361. What would happen if you moved them?

362. If so, how could you do so?

363. What are you assuming that stops you from doing what you want / need to do?

364. What is the biggest obstacle that you are facing?

365. What is the excuse that you have always used for not achieving your goals?

366. What would be a good starting point to begin a different way of doing some things?

367. How big does the block have to be to stop you in your tracks?

368. If you were to break it down, what would the first steps be?

Planning and Metrics

Assists the client in defining key steps to moving forward and understanding how well they are doing.

369. What is worth beginning?

370. What is the first step?

371. When would be the best time to procrastinate about this?

372. What are the pluses and minuses of this situation?

373. How have you handled this situation in the past?

374. Where do you spend most of your energy with this situation?

375. How much planning is enough / good enough?

376. When will enough be good enough?

377. What could you stop doing that would help your situation?

378. What first steps could be taken to give you the confidence to make real progress?

379. What happens if you do nothing?

380. What have you not done?

381. What is the quick fix solution?

382. What is the permanent solution?

383. What are the pros and cons of each?

384. What would be the impact of doing exactly the opposite of what is planned?

385. What would put you back in control?

386. What will you do today that will help take you where you want to be?

387. What did you do today that helped take you where you want to be?

388. What will you think about on the journey to work / home?

389. When is this an issue for you - today / tomorrow?

390. What would you do differently if you felt able to take a more strategic approach?

391. What do you do that you can no longer afford to do in the same way?

392. What is the right amount of risk to take at this point in your career / relationship / project etc.?

393. What are you trying to make happen in the next three months?

394. What has gone really well for you today?

395. How do you measure your success?

396. What would your measurement look like if you used smaller increments?

397. How do you measure the success of others?

398. When you think about your performance, what would need to happen to improve it?

399. What are the costs to your performance?

400. Who else is paying the costs?

401. What will / could you lose by winning?

402. How will you know you're achieving?

403. How did you judge your success in the past?

404. What would be a different way of measuring this?

405. Are you aware of how others measure your success / challenges?

406. How do you visually manage your progress?

407. What daily / weekly routines could you create to show you are succeeding?

Resources

Exploring any one and any thing that can aid and assist the client towards achievement of their goals and outcomes.

408. Who can help?

409. What is it that others can bring?

410. What do you bring to this role?

411. What would be the cost of any immediate actions you could take?

412. Who can give you additional support right now?

413. What would be the most appropriate areas for networking?

414. What could you do more of that would raise your presence?
415. Who else is losing sleep over this?
416. How can you work together to find a resolution?
417. Who could / should you ask for help?
418. What is stopping you from doing so?
419. Who else has a call on your time, your mental energy, your attention?
420. Who else shares ownership of this issue with you?
421. Who else's job are you doing as well as your own?
422. What do you believe will benefit you the most?
423. What or who can assist you getting into action?
424. What could you / do you want to do to change that?
425. Do you know that or believe it?
426. What new relationships do you need to make?
427. What would help you to have more impact?

Setting Targets

Questions to help the client define clear levels of ambition and goals. Gaining clarity around what it is that client is aiming for.

428. What would you achieve by setting realistic targets?
429. By how much do you want to improve?
430. What would be five incremental steps towards this target?
431. Who or what would be your best monitor for achievement?
432. When would you envisage this happening?
433. What contingency would you put in place?
434. How might you sabotage your target?
435. If this was an experiment, what would you expect?

436. What method would you use to achieve this?

437. What conclusions would you draw?

438. How genuinely committed are you to this target?

439. What would need to happen to increase your commitment?

440. What results do you truly want to achieve?

441. If you get that outcome what will that give you?

442. What aspects of your life will be impacted by reaching the target?

443. What is the excuse that you have always used for not achieving your target?

444. What would achievement look / sound / feel like?

445. What would be different so I knew you had achieved it?

446. How does this target impact your spouse / partner / colleagues?

447. What difference will setting this target make?

448. What other goals do you have that might / will take higher priority over this one?

449. Which other goals do you have which are conflicting with this one?

450. Which other goals do you have that are supporting this one?

451. Which other goals do you have which are compatible with this one?

452. Whose targets / goals are these?

453. Who else has a vested interested in you achieving these?

454. How strategic are these targets?

455. How would your targets change, looking at a 5, 10 or even a 20-year time span?

456. How motivated are you to achieving these targets? On a scale 1 - 10?

Team Coaching

> A series of questions that will encourage discussion within teams that can assist the team to identify issues, strengths and challenges.

457. What do you need to stop, start and /or change in the year ahead?
458. What reasons do you have for doing these things?
459. How would you describe a high performing team?
460. What would be your description of this team?
461. What are your thoughts about your team's working strategies on this project?
462. On a scale of 1 to 10 (where 1 is low and 10 is high) how would you rate the performance of this team?
463. What would be your reasons for describing them as 'X'?
464. Think of the best team you have ever been a member of – what was present?
465. Think of the best team you have ever been a member of – what was absent?
466. What are the strengths of this team?
467. What is this team really good at?
468. Where does the team struggle?
469. How does the team struggle?
470. What do other high performing teams exhibit?
471. What are the biggest team opportunities for development?
472. What could threaten the survival of the team?
473. What 3 words would you use to describe this team?
474. What 3 words would you never use to describe this team?
475. How does the team get in the way of itself?
476. What is the main aim or purpose of the team?

477. What does the team need to let go of in order to move forward?
478. What's the team's blind spot?
479. What does the team refuse to confront or address?
480. What are the unspoken norms of the team?
481. How do you succeed as an individual in the team?
482. How does the team react to bad behaviour?
483. How is the 'shadow' of the leader reflected in the team?
484. How diverse are the skills / competencies in this team?
485. How does that help or hinder the team's performance?
486. What does the team need to spend more time on?
487. What does the team need to spend less time on?
488. What are the 'right' things for the team to be working on?
489. Where is the team focussing on the 'wrong' things?
490. Who does this team rely on or need to work with to achieve its ambition?
491. How flexible or adaptable is the team?
492. How resilient is the team?
493. What would make it more resilient?
494. How does learning occur in the team?
495. How does the team accommodate new people?
496. How does the team celebrate success?
497. How does the team learn from its mistakes?
498. How does the team come to terms with losing team members?
499. What does this team need to do differently?
500. How can this team adapt more quickly and move swiftly?
501. What is the system at work here?
502. What is the elephant in the room?
503. What is the bigger picture?

Vision and Purpose

These are questions which enable the client to articulate an inspiring future.

504. What is your vision of yourself as a leader?
505. What will you realise in a year's time that you already knew today?
506. What do you want to believe about this?
507. What are the risks of success?
508. What have you done today to help make a dream a reality?
509. What is in the best interests of the team / customer / future / next generation?
510. What would you most want to develop if there were no constraints?
511. What changes would you make if you were able?
512. Where will you be in three and five years' time?
513. What would be your top three priorities at this time?
514. What will be different when you have your solution?
515. What will you see / hear / feel as you walk the corridor?
516. What do you want the outcome to be?
517. What do you want to become?
518. What is your greatest ambition?
519. What does the gap between success and failure look like?
520. How does your work help you fulfil your life purpose?
521. Where is your work in conflict with your life purpose?
522. What inspires you (about this)?
523. Who in this organisation thinks like a customer?
524. Why isn't it you?

525. If you look five years into the future, how did your leadership change the way things work around here?

526. If you were to develop more skills necessary for a strategic leadership role, what would you stand to lose in your present role?

527. What would you stand to gain in your present role?

528. What would you be doing differently?

529. What is in the best interests of the team / customer / future / next generation?

530. What is your relationship with your organization / institution?

531. What is it telling you now?

532. What questions would you most like to be asked about your role / organisation / department?

533. What questions would you least like to be asked about your role / organisation / department?

534. What was it about this company that made you join?

535. How does this organisation fit with your mission / purpose?

536. What does this job give you that you wouldn't otherwise have?

537. What do you value most in work?

538. What was it that you did or said that made your company want to bring you on board?

539. How does what you do differ from what your job description says you do?

540. To what extent does this job help you achieve your career goals?

541. What do you want to be known for?

542. What are you prepared to do to create the future you want?

543. What is the best possible job anyone could offer you right now / two years' time?

544. When will you begin to create this future?

My Favourite Questions

Chapter 8
Change

Contents:

Beliefs

> Beliefs are the principles /rules / assumptions that guide our
> actions, they are our reality and we act upon them.
> Questions that challenge them can enable reflection and
> cause change; moving the client forward into a different,
> more positive action.

1. What is true about this?

2. What are you willing to change about this belief?

3. What else could you choose to believe?

4. What other perspectives are there?

5. Have you always believed that?

6. When have you believed differently?

7. What rules might you be running here?

8. What other possibilities are there?

9. Do you have a belief about what 'should be' in this situation?

10. What other ways are there of considering the issue?

11. What if you were to consider a different belief?

12. What would that do for you?

13. Could you generate several other possible beliefs that could influence how you act in this situation?

14. If this alternative belief were true, what might you notice?

15. Which belief would be most useful to you as you think about moving into action?

16. What steps do you want to take?

17. What is next?

18. What do you believe the plan to be?

19. What would make you ready to commit to this plan of action?

20. What will you do?

21. What do you currently believe about this issue / situation?

22. How does this belief influence you and your decisions?

23. How would you describe it?

24. What is really true about this issue / situation?

25. What would enable you to question the validity of this belief?

26. What would cause some doubt in your mind about this assumption?

27. As you think of a time when you first began to question an old belief, what was happening then?

28. What would happen if you could 'map' that across to the beliefs currently holding you back?

29. What would happen if you could store old beliefs away – where would you put them?

30. How would you label them?

31. What new belief would serve you better at this point?

32. What would you rather be doing?

33. How would you state your desired belief?

34. What would need to happen for you to know that this new belief is true?

35. What would enable you to be open to believing something different from your current belief?
36. When will you be ready to embrace a new belief?
37. What are your most dearly held beliefs?
38. Which of those serve you well and which do not?
39. What would life be like if you held the new belief as dearly?
40. What have you believed that limits you?
41. What assumptions have you been making that are no longer valid?
42. What is 'challenging / not working / perfect' about this?
43. What do you need to believe about yourself that will support you?
44. How will you know that to be true?
45. What are your 'rules' about consistency / loyalty?
46. When do they keep you in a rut?
47. What 'rules' are you using that could be challenged?
48. How would you like them challenged?
49. If you could have this right now, on a plate, would you take it?
50. What might be useful to believe?
51. What is important about this story?
52. What did you learn from that experience?
53. What is really holding you back?
54. What is the cost of worrying about this?
55. What chasm requires a big step to cross it?
56. What would that step be?
57. What could that step be?
58. When could that step be taken?
59. What is the risk if you change?

60. And what is the risk if you do not change?

61. What are you doing to change this situation?

62. What question do you hear me asking you right now?

63. What do you want to believe about the future?

64. What do you care about as you think about your change?

65. What would enable you to be confident that you can shift a belief?

66. How will you begin this shift?

67. How would I know you shifted?

Capability

This section suggests questions that could stretch the client to build new capabilities / skills; increasing their confidence to change and do things differently or better than before.

68. What would be a stretch for you?

69. What do you consider beyond your ability?

70. How can you change that?

71. What would happen if you tried to go beyond this thinking?

72. Where have you put your bar?

73. How could you raise the bar for yourself?

74. When have you achieved above your own bar?

75. What would be an even bigger goal?

76. What is the highest you could aspire to?

77. What relevant qualities and skills do you already have?

78. How can you apply them to the current situation?

79. What else do you need?

80. How will you create that?

81. If you had to live with just yourself for three months, how would it be by the end?

82. What would you change?

83. What would you build upon?

84. What wouldn't happen if you did?

85. What would happen if you did?

86. What wouldn't happen if you didn't?

87. What would happen if you didn't?

88. What is the worst thing that could happen if you did 'X'?

89. What is the best thing that could happen if you did 'X'?

90. What is the worst thing that could happen if you didn't do 'X'?

91. What is the best thing that could happen if you didn't do 'X'?

92. What do you already contribute to the success of your team / organisation?

93. What more can you do?

94. What can you contribute towards the success of the group / team / organisation?

95. How will you come alive this week?

96. How do you learn to trust movement?

97. When does movement turn into momentum?

98. How do you squander your energy on what is not real, only imagined?

99. How much time is spent wondering how it could have been different?

100. Where do you think 'what if' is not fair or right?

101. How can you be willing to have it so?

102. How will you know if things are going well?

103. How could you find peace with your current situation?

104. How could you substitute one for the other?

105. What has to shift in your thinking about this?

106. What do you want to happen?

107. What is the crucial conversation you need to have to change the predicament and with whom?

108. When will you be willing to ask the challenging questions?

109. What do you need to develop this skill?

110. Who would champion you on this journey?

111. What would you be prepared to ask them?

112. When will you make this ask?

Getting into Action

Assisting the client to explore what makes things worthwhile for them. These questions enable the client to move from 'thinking about it' into action. They also challenge the client, at a deeper level, to drive themselves forward.

113. What motivates you right now?

114. What excites you in the morning?

115. What is worth getting out of bed for?

116. What is currently preventing you from reaching your goal?

117. What can you eliminate in your life to help you reach your goal this time?

118. What do you need to add to your life?

119. What are you tolerating right now in your business and personal life?

120. What are you willing to do in the next 30 days?

121. When will you start?

122. What is really important to you – rather than merely urgent?

123. What is your underlying purpose here?

124. What are you not noticing that needs attention?

125. If you were an objective observer of yourself, what would you now notice?
126. If you viewed things from another person's point of view, what new information would that perspective give you?
127. How would that knowledge get you into action?
128. What do you need to do differently?
129. What do you need to do more of?
130. What do you need to do less of?
131. How are you directing your thinking in a useful direction?
132. What will be the most productive direction for your thinking?
133. What do you want to create?
134. What do you really need?
135. What is your heart telling you?
136. What is your head telling you?
137. What is important now?
138. What ought to happen?
139. Where do you want to be in 5 or 10 years from now?
140. What action are you taking toward that?
141. What does this mean to you?
142. And if you achieved that, what would that do for you?
143. When is good, good enough?
144. On a scale of 1 – 10 how happy would achieving this goal / outcome make you?
145. What is most important to you?
146. What do you really want?
147. If you had enough support, what is the largest change you'd like to make in your business / life?
148. Where will you find this support?
149. What do you crave / desire / long for?

150. What would you like to create?

151. On a scale of 1 – 10 how important is it?

152. If you only had six, perfectly healthy, months to live, what would you do now?

153. What would it take to have your ideal day?

154. What would your ideal day / life / moment be like?

155. How are you planning to get there?

156. What is missing here?

157. If a friend / colleague was in a similar situation what would you say to them?

158. Which of your behaviours could get in the way of the change?

159. What is the positive intention behind this behaviour?

160. What, in this situation, can you be grateful for?

161. What are you experiencing / thinking / feeling about this situation?

162. What do you think others are experiencing in this situation?

163. How much energy do you have for this?

164. On a scale of 1 – 10, how compelled are you to do this?

165. What could be your first step?

166. How will you do that?

167. Is a change worth making?

168. What would be the benefits?

169. How committed are you to making a change on a scale of 1-10?

170. What will get you started?

171. What kind of plan do you want to make?

172. How will you monitor your progress?

173. What action could you take to improve this situation?

174. Are you happy with the way things are going?

175. If not, what are you going to do about it?

176. When will you take this action?

177. What is the most useful thing you could do right now to take you where you want to go?

178. What action will make the greatest difference?

179. What is your next step?

180. What changes do you need to initiate?

181. How will you initiate those changes?

182. What about the costs of changing – what are your plans to manage these?

183. What is the cost of not taking action?

184. If your life depended on taking action, what would you do?

185. What are you doing currently that you would like to change now or in the future?

186. What will you let go of in order to have these changes?

187. What is getting in the way of starting that change now?

188. How different would it be if you were to plan the start after this session?

189. What could be your stepping-stones?

190. What do you currently do that makes you shine?

191. How can you do more?

192. What gives you joy, a sense of satisfaction and energy?

193. What areas drain and deplete you, and could be delegated?

194. Where is your fulfilment?

195. What is the very first thing to do?

196. What would you place importance on?

197. What would create an impact?

198. What would be different if those were happening now?

199. What would you need to do to start things happening?

200. How often would you do this?

201. What would be necessary to do this?

202. How could it not be onerous?

203. What conversations do you need to have and with whom?

204. What will you acknowledge about yourself after today's session?

205. What would the ideal outcome for your situation / issue be?

206. What do you notice about your direction over the past week, month, year?

207. In what direction are you moving now?

208. What could cause you to change direction?

209. If you were to tell me about the journey you're going on, what would it look / sound / feel like?

210. What will you do to manage your energy levels on this journey?

211. What will you do to pick yourself up?

Identity

This section begins to allow your client to find out who they are and how they want to exist in the world around them. Identity is finding out who you take yourself to be. Further suggested questions are located in Chapter 10, Client Identity starting on page 161.

212. Who are you being?

213. If you are not being you, who is?

214. What really matters?

215. What do you want your legacy to be?

216. Who do you want to be in this situation?
217. Who do you want to show up as?
218. How willing are you to do whatever it takes to discover the highest and best of who you are?
219. What are the underlying assumptions that you are making about yourself?
220. Are those assumptions supporting you?
221. How will you step into being your true you?
222. What is your calling?
223. How will you pursue it?
224. What does your 'blind eye' see?
225. What is it to trust yourself?
226. What is your life really about?
227. What is your purpose?
228. What is it to live fully?
229. How will the true you 'live' out loud?
230. How will you be an artist in the world?
231. What quality of thought do you sacrifice under duress?
232. When don't you trust how you will act?
233. What 'you' might show up?
234. If, at the end of the day, you felt you had become a better person, what would have happened to you?
235. When did you last feel content with yourself?
236. When you are 95 years old, what will you want to say about your life?
237. What will you think about this five years from now?
238. How does this relate to your life purpose?
239. In the bigger scheme of things, how important is this?
240. What would happen, or might happen if you were to change?

241. What would you need to know about yourself, to know that you've taken full responsibility for this change?

242. Which of your innate skills could you bring to this situation?

243. How will you become who you want to be?

244. How can you effect the change?

245. What choices do you have right now?

246. Who do others see?

247. When will you know you are being your authentic self?

Letting Go

These questions can enable an exploration of what the client is holding onto that may not serve them so well. Not letting go may get in the way of change. It also begins to explore what the 'cost' maybe of having or not having certain behaviours / issues.

248. Is letting go of this an option?

249. What is the cost to you of playing it safe?

250. Which dreams did you let go of?

251. What dreams can you reconnect with?

252. What part of yourself are you leaving behind?

253. If you were not concerned about what anyone else thought, what would you keep / let go of?

254. What have you not tried because you were concerned about looking good?

255. If it were completely safe, what would you risk changing?

256. How can you ensure a sense of safety as you take a risky step?

257. What would be the safe choice?

258. What would be the daring choice?

259. What do you fear might happen?

260. What would you need to cope with that?

261. What would it take for you to overcome your fears and take action to change?

262. What support do you want from me as your coach as you begin to let go of this issue?

263. Are you being productive or just active?

264. What will you do differently?

265. When will you do it?

266. How will you be accountable?

267. If there were no constraints, what would you change?

268. If you suspended doubt and worry, what actions would you take?

269. How will you let go of it?

270. What is the cost of letting go?

271. What is the cost of not letting go?

272. What will you gain by letting go?

273. What is the real change you want to make?

274. What would I see / hear you doing differently?

Options

This section explores what alternatives may exist for your client. It can also invite the client to understand some of their experiences from a different perspective thereby creating new meanings.

275. What important choices are available to you now?

276. In five years' time what decision will you be glad you had made now?

277. Is the direction you are moving in one you have chosen?

278. If not, which direction would you have chosen?

279. What other choices do you have?

280. Which option best fits your goals?

281. What are your options?

282. How will you find the courage to move beyond your comfort zone?

283. What is possible?

284. What could you do that you think is impossible?

285. What if it works out exactly as you want it to be?

286. What do you choose to dream?

287. What is exciting to you about this?

288. What is the urge?

289. What does your intuition tell you?

290. If you had free choice in the matter, what would you do?

291. If the same thing came up again, what would you do differently?

292. If we could wipe the slate clean today, what would you clean?

293. If you had it to do over again, what would you keep?

294. What else would best serve you at this time?

295. What does this situation mean to you?

296. What might it mean to others?

297. How might other people see it?

298. How will it appear to you in three years' time?

299. How did you get here?

300. What are the benefits of it being as it is now?

301. What do you get from it being this way?

302. How does it being like this help?

303. How does it being like this hinder?

304. What would be better than this?

305. What would be even better still?

306. What did you do to get this way?

307. What causes it?

308. What drives it?

309. How is it a function of the system in which you operate?

310. Who are the key players in this environment / system?

311. What other environments / systems do you operate in?

312. How do these environments / systems interact?

313. If you feel that you don't have other options, what would happen if you did?

314. If you did have choices, what might they be?

315. What would be the most useful question for me to ask you next?

316. If you carry on as you are, will you reach your goals in the time you've given yourself?

317. What options do you need in order to get where you want to go?

318. What options do you want?

319. What will they be like?

320. What is stopping you exploring the other options?

321. What will happen if you do explore?

322. What will happen if you don't do this?

323. What won't happen if you do this?

324. Which path do you want to take?

325. Which path would be the easiest one to take?

326. Which would be the best?

327. In which direction could you go instead?

328. How wide is the path you are travelling?

329. If you made a detour where would that take you?

Procrastination

These questions refer to investigating your client's action of making low-priority tasks more important than high-priority ones. Exploring what causes the putting off of important tasks and your client's strategy for avoidance.

330. How will waiting serve you?
331. How much energy are you spending on avoiding this job?
332. How are you avoiding it?
333. What is the positive intent of the part that is causing the procrastination?
334. What is a realistic assessment of the time it will take?
335. How would you break this down into smaller tasks?
336. What kind of timeline do you want to follow to get through this project?
337. Is there someone you can delegate this task to?
338. What parts of this task could be delegated?
339. How much do you really need to control?
340. What would others gain if you were to share or delegate?
341. What do you need to do to make it happen?
342. What stops you?
343. If you were to know, what would it be?
344. What will that look like?
345. How did you get there?
346. What would happen if you did it?
347. What would happen if you didn't do it?
348. What wouldn't happen if you did it?
349. What wouldn't happen if you didn't do it?
350. What are you afraid of?
351. What would you get that you're not getting now?

352. What would you need to do to get clearer?

353. What resources did you use before?

354. What action is most aligned with your values?

355. How will you vote for what really needs doing?

356. What will sustain you as you make the journey into action?

357. If you were to put yourself first, what would your decision be?

358. What do you want for yourself?

359. If you felt you could be totally selfish, what would you do?

360. What is 100% of what you want in this situation?

361. How could you get some more of what will satisfy you?

362. How could you say no to these requests that drain you?

363. Where do you want to draw boundaries?

364. Is where you are now closer to where you want to be?

365. What do you need to do next?

366. What is your general sense of direction?

367. Are you going towards what you want to achieve or being blown off course?

368. What could be blowing you off course?

369. What would pull you back on course?

370. What would positively stretch you now?

371. What do you make of it?

372. What do you think is best?

373. How does it look to you?

374. How do you feel about it?

375. What resonates for you?

376. What are the possibilities?

377. If you had your choice, what would you do?

378. What are possible solutions?

379. What will happen if you try to implement them?

380. What will happen if you don't?

381. What options can you create?

382. What crutch is a comfort for you?

383. If this issue wasn't there to keep you busy, what would be?

Chapter 9
Career and Transitioning

Contents:

Beliefs

> Beliefs are the principles / rules / assumptions that guide our actions, they inform our reality and we act upon them. Questions that challenge them can enable reflection and cause change; moving the client forward into a different, more positive action.

1. What do you believe about role / career?

2. What do you believe about yourself in this situation?

3. What do you believe others think when they think of you?

4. What are the different parts of you?

5. What is the intention of each of those parts?

6. How do those parts come together?

7. What is it that you believe about this situation?

8. How would you know if that wasn't true?

9. What enables this situation to persist?

10. What assumptions are you making about it?

11. How might your assumptions be contributing to the situation?

12. How is that an issue for you?

13. What will it mean for your life / career if you don't believe 'X'?

14. What will be different about the way in which you see yourself if you believe 'X'?

15. How does that fit in with where you want to be?

16. What is the worst thing that could happen?

17. What is the best thing that could happen?

18. What is possible with taking the next step?

19. If you take this step, what would you do next?

20. What is the gift in this challenge?

21. What can you control in this situation?

22. How will it feel to do that?

23. What can't you control in the situation?

24. What do you believe is possible for you?

25. What do you believe is getting in your way?

26. What might you control that you haven't been able to in the past?

27. How do you know the difference?

28. What would you like most to be acknowledged for so far in your career?

29. If you were your own coach, what would you say to yourself right now?

30. What, in this situation, can you find to be grateful for?

31. What are you going to do differently tomorrow?

32. How will you summarise what you are going to do and by when?

33. What will you be known for at your work?

34. What do you believe you can truly achieve?

35. What beliefs would best suit you?

Fears

This section is about enabling your client to identify their fears, what really gets in their own way. The distressing emotions aroused by perceived impending risk can be debilitating whether real or imagined.

36. What major fear will you be addressing if you 'X'?
37. What 'magic solution' would make that fear decrease / disappear?
38. How do you do that?
39. What do you need to make this happen?
40. What would you try now if you knew you could not fail?
41. What do you need to you make that 'magic solution' become reality?
42. What makes that important to you?
43. Where do you know you are stopping short?
44. How is that working for you?
45. What other options can you think of?
46. What is the simple answer to this?
47. What resources would you need to enable you to step back and view this less fearfully?
48. How will you summon the courage to follow through with the actions that are right?
49. What will sustain you as you make this potentially unpopular decision?
50. What will you report back to me when you have taken this scary step?
51. What is 'good enough' for you right now?
52. What is the consequence of making the wrong decision or coming to the wrong conclusion?

53. What is the consequence of making the right decision or coming to the right conclusion?
54. What would make you feel most empowered in this situation?
55. What needs to become clear for you?
56. And if you were to know what is clear for you – what would that do?
57. What if you knew everything you need know?
58. What would you do / say / think?
59. How does fear of criticism effect your actions?
60. What do you do to enlist feedback?
61. How will you summon the courage to follow through with the action you know is right for you?

One Hundred Day Plans

Questions to provoke exploration of the client's aims, goals and objectives during a transition phase and enable them to be effective during that first period in the new role. The results of their actions will really begin to become evident after 100 days.

62. How will you plan your first days / weeks?
63. What key skills / attributes will you bring along with you?
64. What do you want to achieve within your first 100 days?
65. What is important to achieve first?
66. How will you map your priorities?
67. Who do you need to enable / help you to achieve it?
68. What will achieving it do for you?
69. What would be balance for you in this new role?

70. How important is it for you to maintain this balance in your new role?
71. What do you want others to see you doing?
72. How will you communicate this?
73. What do you want to be as you hit this particular transition phase?
74. How could that be improved?
75. How will making this transition / move affect that balance?
76. What will be the consequences of the changes?
77. How could you maintain balance within your planning?
78. What do you plan to do about it?
79. What is your game plan?
80. What would be a good starting point?
81. What will enable you to engage others?
82. What will you do?
83. If there were 5 key steps over this period, what would they be?
84. What kind of plan do you need to create?
85. What do you need to do to hit the ground running?
86. How will you know when you have reached your 100-day goal?
87. What will you see, hear, feel with achievement?
88. How much effort do you need to put in before and during this phase?
89. What do you need to let go of in order to achieve your plan?
90. How could it be effortless?
91. Who will be impacted by your plan?
92. What will you do to mitigate any upheaval?
93. What will others say about you on day 101?

Outcomes

> The outcome is always where your client is headed and it sets the direction for taking the appropriate actions. It focuses their attention on what they are ultimately aiming for.

94. When are you working at your best?
95. What skills would you prefer to be using?
96. What will you do to develop them?
97. What would you most like to develop in yourself?
98. What skills do you believe are fully transferable?
99. Which of these do you feel confident about?
100. Which other industries would you like to consider?
101. Who would you love to be working with?
102. What organisation would be your dream place to work?
103. What will you do to move towards that?
104. What kind of working structure do you prefer?
105. How does that differ from your current role / situation?
106. What kind of location suits you best?
107. What would be a stretch for you now?
108. What would take you outside your comfort zone?
109. What stretch would you agree to?
110. What is your ideal working environment?
111. What would be your dream role / job?
112. What would you need to begin your ambition?
113. What kind of journey would you like to be on over the next few years?
114. How do you experience failures and mistakes?
115. How do you learn from them?

116. From your list of priorities, which would be your top outcome?

117. What steps would you need to begin to take to achieve that outcome?

118. When would be a good time to start?

119. How does the outcome of that task / goal / action fit with your values?

120. What will you have achieved from your career in one, two, five years' time?

Procrastination

These questions refer to investigating your client's action of making low-priority tasks more important than high-priority ones. Exploring what causes the putting off of important tasks and your client's strategy for avoidance.

121. How do you get in your own way?

122. What will you start doing now to make that (activity / goal) happen?

123. What is stopping you doing that?

124. Are you ready to make and commit to a decision now?

125. When does commitment not turn into action?

126. What is at play then?

127. What questions should you ask yourself before our next meeting to make good use of our next coaching session?

128. What is the most useful thing you could do right now?

129. What exactly do you want?

130. If you were to apply the 80/20 rule to this situation, how would that change it?

131. Which tasks would have the most serious consequences (positive or negative) on your career if you were to deliver them?
132. So, what is holding you back from doing them?
133. If you were to organise your 'to do' list by value and priority which would you start on?
134. Which tasks are most important to enabling you to get your job done or move ahead in your career?
135. What are you particularly good at doing?
136. What is it about them that makes you good?
137. How about starting on those then?
138. Where are the bottlenecks or choke points in this project / situation?
139. Which time of day are you at your most effective?
140. What could be the first step to operating around those times?
141. Imagine you had to leave town at the end of the week and work as if you had to get all your major tasks completed before you left – which ones are the tasks you would most want to complete?
142. What gets in the way of the other tasks?
143. If you were your own cheerleader what would you say / sing / shout?
144. Which is the most difficult task to complete?
145. What could make them easy?
146. Would you prefer to do that first or last?
147. How did you decide that?
148. If you were to break this down into smaller chunks how would you do that?
149. Where would you start?

150. Which chunk would you begin with?

151. When would you start that?

152. If you need a larger chunk of time when could you schedule that?

153. If you had to make a decision now, what would that be?

154. What is the worst thing that could happen if you did not?

155. What is the best thing that could happen if you did not?

156. Who are you being when you hesitate?

Reflections

> Questions from this section allows your client to take some time to experience and understand their journey so far.

157. If you think of your working life as a journey, what sort of journey has it been so far?

158. What new things have you done over the last year?

159. What outstanding things have you done over the last year?

160. What have you done over the last year that you can celebrate right now?

161. What learning do you want to carry forward?

162. How will you celebrate your achievements?

163. How did you honour your passions?

164. To what extent do you live your passions?

165. What did you project about yourself this time last year / last week?

166. Is your life congruent with your passions?

167. To what extent are you spending your time in areas that make full use of your talents?

168. To what extent do you have the knowledge necessary to pursue your path with ease?

169. What are you doing to increase your effective knowledge?

170. When you think about your current or next role, what are the things you would most like to do?

171. What did you 'get' from your last important role?

172. To what extent is your reputation attractive to others?

173. Thinking about your qualities, what are you doing to promote them so people who know you / know of you, know who you really are?

174. What is your purpose?

175. To what extent are you clearly living your life purpose?

176. What will having that goal / belief / decision give you or allow you to have?

177. What is your calling?

178. How will you pursue it?

179. What are you becoming as you wake and sleep?

180. How does your character show up in a crisis?

181. How do you learn best?

182. How did you foster your own development?

183. What were the most challenging and exciting career development opportunities that you have experienced?

Reframing

> Questions to enable your client to find alternative ways of reviewing and understanding what has happened in the past. Creating the possibility of new meanings and thereby changing the impact of past events / actions.

184. What else could this experience mean?

185. What is the positive value of this experience?

186. How else could this experience be described?

187. What does this look / feel like from someone else's eyes?

188. What would enable you to change what they see or hear?

189. What is important about that for you?

190. What would you gain?

191. What aspect of this experience could provide a different meaning?

192. Is there a larger frame in which this experience could have a positive value?

193. What would that larger frame look like?

194. How is that a problem/issue for you?

195. What are the positive and negative consequences?

196. What would your role model / mentor do in this situation?

197. How will this situation look 6 months / one year / 5 years from now?

198. If you were able to see yourself in this situation, what would you see?

199. What would you do if you were your boss / partner / parent?

200. What would it be like to be in their shoes?

201. Suppose you had more information, how would that change what you thought about this situation?

202. What would that information / knowledge be?

203. What would you do with that knowledge?

204. How could that change your circumstances?

205. If you were to wave a magic wand what would change?

206. If there was a metaphor for this experience, what would it be?

207. If you were to change that to a different metaphor, what would it be?

208. How would that change your view of that experience?

Success

This section explores how your client characterises success and what it means to them. It helps to set the scene for future successful actions.

209. What is success for you now?
210. What would you classify as your most successful moments?
211. What made them happen?
212. What can you celebrate about yourself?
213. What actions can you take to change this to make it more successful?
214. Success according to whom?
215. What is the cost to you / others of you being successful?
216. What would comprise your success?
217. What would they need to do be on your team?
218. How do you know when you have achieved your goals?
219. How do you know when you are on / off track?
220. What do you do to achieve your goals?
221. What actions do you take / can you take?
222. What would you need to do to take more action?
223. What actions do you need to let go of in order to be successful?
224. What do you do when you are off track or not achieving your desired results?
225. How do you respond to the situation, internally and externally?
226. How would things have to be set up for you to be extremely successful without changing anything at all?
227. What is your ultimate success?

228. To what extent does your success relate to your life purpose?
229. How do you define success in your future?
230. How have you previously defined success?
231. How would you define happiness?
232. If you were receiving recognition for your success, how would that make you feel?
233. What are you supposed to achieve?
234. Who would you be to be truly successful in your eyes?
235. What do you want to achieve?
236. What is success in your eyes and the eyes of others?
237. What are you moving towards?
238. What is keeping you small?
239. What would enable you to be big?
240. How are you holding yourself small?
241. How small would big have to be?
242. What would enable you to grow?
243. What is it like living in your world?
244. What would you do differently?
245. What would it be like if you were one of the people you most admired?
246. Consider your future vision of your career path, where would you like to be in one, two, five, ten years' time?
247. How will you have made a difference?
248. How will things be different for you?
249. What do you notice?
250. What would you like to do more of?
251. Who does success well?
252. What do others do?
253. How will you develop more of those skills?

Values

These questions elicit what is truly important to your client. They are unique to your client, the qualities that define them and help them make choices. Values relate to principles rather morals and are why we do what we do.

254. What is important to you?

255. What is important to you about your career / job?

256. What is it about that which makes it important?

257. When did you decide that was important?

258. What matters most to you?

259. What really annoys you?

260. What is it about that which causes you to feel that way?

261. What have been the highs / lows in your career to date?

262. What made them stand out?

263. What was the emotion that was happening at that time?

264. How did you use that emotion?

265. With hindsight, what would you have preferred to have happened?

266. What would you change / keep the same?

267. What would your top five values be?

268. How are your values being / not being honoured in your current role?

269. How does this role / career move match against / honour your values?

270. How would the role / career you are considering match with your top 5 values?

271. What about the others?

272. What is missing?

273. How important is that to you?

274. If you had all your values present in your work, what would make you leave it?
275. What inspires you?
276. What challenges you?
277. What encourages you?
278. How certain are you of your conviction to your values?
279. What gives you the courage to continue in times of uncertainty and adversity?

My Favourite Questions

Chapter 10
Client Identity

Contents:

Clarity of Passion

> These questions encourage the client to get clearer about what they want – what really inspires and drives them. Clarity can enable them to focus their energy in the right direction for them.

1. What are your passions?

2. To what extent do you live your passions?

3. How do you project your passions?

4. What is it that makes you get up in the morning?

5. What is it that makes you want to stay in bed in the mornings?

6. How do you use your leisure time?

7. What would you rather be doing?

8. What inspires you?

9. Who do you know who loves what they do?

10. What is it that they are engaging with?

11. What is it that you would like to engage with?

12. What past passions have you lost touch with?

13. What would it be like to reconnect with your passions?

14. What did you love doing when you were 7, 18, 24 years old?

15. If you could be doing anything, what would you choose?

16. When have you been so absorbed that you lose track of time?
17. What were you doing?
18. When do you compromise?
19. When is compromise appropriate?
20. When is compromise out of alignment with who you are?
21. When is compromise out of alignment with what you believe in?
22. What would be a first step to making your passion come alive?

Creating a Self

'Creating a self' questions are for enquiring into who your client is being – how well they know themselves and what is really important to them.

23. Who are you becoming?
24. Who would you like to become?
25. What are the incremental steps you have taken this week that are creating the you of the future?
26. How is this action shaping who you are?
27. How do you give yourself a rest when you know you really need one?
28. What do you need to acknowledge yourself for?
29. What deserves celebration?
30. What does success look / sound / feel like?
31. Who are you?
32. Who will you be when you achieve 'X'?
33. What will others see in you?
34. If you are not being you, who is, and who are you being?

35. Who do you want to be in this situation?
36. Who do you want to show up as?
37. Who is in control?
38. Who decides?
39. As you move forwards, what do you notice about who you are becoming?
40. What is mastery?
41. What will you do to achieve it?
42. When are you impatient with your progress?
43. How do you dance in life when you don't know all the steps?
44. What part of you wants clarity?
45. What will you do in order to get clarity?
46. How will you step into your purpose?
47. At 90, what will you wish you had tried?
48. What kind of character do you want to forge?
49. What choices have forged your character recently?
50. What will you do efficiently that is not really important to you?
51. What is really important to you?
52. What calls you deeply?
53. What if the question at the Pearly Gates is 'did you have a good time'? What will you say?
54. A seemingly random mix of events and experiences are unique to you - what themes emerge?
55. What exists nowhere but within you?
56. How did you show up today?
57. How are you showing up right now?
58. If you had only yourself for company, what kind of company would you be?

59. How could gratefulness or curiosity become the channel your thoughts flow into?

60. What other channels would you like to create?

61. What wisdom do you give to your friends and family?

62. How can you be that wise with yourself?

63. How can you be that gentle with yourself?

64. Visit yourself at 90, in good health, having lived a satisfying life: what do you notice?

65. What self are you growing into?

66. What does your 'blind eye' see?

67. What is it to trust yourself?

68. What provokes you to try to fit in, to be 'like them'?

69. How does that behaviour protect you?

70. What is the cost?

71. What learning stimulates your curiosity?

72. What will you reap in quieter years?

73. What is your purpose in life?

74. Which dreams did you let go of?

75. What is your life really about?

76. What inspires you about you?

77. What would you do now if you were already the person you are hoping to become?

78. What was it in you that enabled you to take that step?

79. If you were to put yourself first, what would your decision be?

80. What do you want for yourself?

81. If you felt you could be totally selfish, what would you do?

82. What is 100% of what you want in this situation?

83. How could you get some more of what will satisfy you?

84. What is the self you want to create?

85. What did you do today that expressed your abilities and gave you energy?

86. What drained you?

87. What is the cost to you of playing safe?

88. If you were not concerned about what anyone else thought, what would you do?

89. What have you not tried because you were concerned about looking good?

90. If it were completely safe, what would you risk?

91. If you couldn't fail what would you do?

92. How can you anchor a sense of safety as you take this step?

93. What would be the safe choice?

94. What would be the daring choice?

95. What do you fear might happen?

96. What would you do in order to cope with that?

97. What would it take for you to overcome your fears and take action?

98. What support do you want from me?

99. If you had to live with yourself for three months, how would it be by the end?

100. Is the life you are living worth what you are giving up in order to have it?

101. How would you like to be?

102. How fully engaged with life are you on a scale of 1 – 10?

103. When will you adopt your own style?

104. What are the risks of success of just being you?

105. From where or what do you derive your energy?

106. If you felt you had become a better person, what would have happened to you?

107. Who are you trying to avoid being like?

108. What would you like to believe about yourself?

109. What do you avoid admitting to yourself?

110. Who do you compare yourself with?

111. Who would you prefer to compare yourself with and why?

112. What do you know about yourself?

113. What do you not know about yourself?

114. What captures the essence of you?

115. What does fun mean to you?

116. What was humorous about the situation?

117. How can you make this more fun?

118. How do you want it to be?

119. If you were to teach people how to have fun, what would you say?

120. If you were 'X', what would you be doing that you are not doing now?

Enquiries

These questions are most useful to leave with your client, perhaps at the end of a session. They encourage deeper reflections and some additional self-discovery between coaching sessions.

121. What is it to have a full, rich life?

122. What are you tolerating?

123. Where are you not being realistic?

124. What is integrity?

125. How do you operate?

126. What is it to live in alignment with your values?

127. What is it to be powerful?

128. What is it to be present?

129. What is your prevalent mood?

130. What do your habits say about you?

131. What is choice?

132. What is it to choose?

133. When is it okay to change your mind on something you have given your word on?

134. What is the difference between a wish and a goal?

135. Are you being nice or are you being real?

136. What do you use to avoid feelings? (e.g. alcohol, food, work)

137. Where is your attention - self, others, work, daydreams, vision, values and complaints?

138. Who did you have to be to reach this place?

139. Who have you become?

140. What have you built?

141. What is it to live your life fully?

142. What is it to love deeply?

143. What is your contribution to the world going to be?

144. What values require your complete attention?

145. How can you be yourself while adapting to others' needs?

Looking Back

This Looking Back section encourages the client to start reviewing / reflecting on where have they been and what have they learnt. It helps to identify particular areas of learning that can be carried forward.

146. In what ways have you shaped your life to date?

147. When you look back, what were the key moments?

148. When did you not take a risk?

149. What did you do that played it safe?

150. What do you feel about taking risks?

151. What themes or patterns do you see in your life?

152. What is the greatest achievement of your life and why?

153. How much effort on your part did it require?

154. When have you achieved something without much effort?

155. What does success mean in your life today?

156. What are your previous greatest?

157. What was special about them?

158. Why are they important to you?

159. What excited you about your past / present roles?

160. When have you taken a stand in your life?

161. What was the outcome of taking that stand?

162. How did it make you feel to take a stand?

163. When were you at your most creative / inspired / inspiring / committed / passionate / decisive?

164. What attracted you to each of the roles you have undertaken?

165. What is missing from your current roles / jobs?

166. What was missing from your previous roles / jobs?

Purpose

This section deals with helping your client identify and understand their sense of purpose. These questions can assist the discovery of what gives your client meaningfulness in work and life generally.

167. How would you describe your life purpose today?

168. Whose choices resulted in the life you are now living?

169. What differs from your earlier years?
170. Where would be a good place to start to describe what impact you would like to have on the world?
171. What impact would you like to have around you?
172. If this could be described as a metaphor – what would it be?
173. What really rings true for you?
174. What would happen if your purpose and passion combined?
175. What would that require to really happen?
176. If you could see yourself in the future, what impact would you have had?
177. How did you transform yourself and others around you?
178. What did you do that enabled transformation?
179. Who will you be in the future that you are not being now?
180. What steps did you take on your journey?
181. What were your big decisions?
182. How did you make them?
183. Who journeyed with you?
184. What would you need to happen now that would enable you to live your purpose?
185. Who could you share this with?
186. What will be different in living your purpose?
187. What benefits would be generated through living your purpose?
188. To what extent are you spending your time in areas that make full use of your talents?
189. To what extent do you have the knowledge necessary to pursue your path with ease?
190. What are you doing to increase your effective knowledge?

191. To what extent do you enjoy the reputation you have?

192. What would you like your reputation to be?

193. What are you doing to create that?

194. What will having a purpose allow you to have?

Who Are You Being?

This section is all about exploring your client's identity; how they really see themselves and how their actions reflect the person they are being.

195. When you are being you, who is that?

196. What is your vision of you?

197. What will help you live the life you want?

198. How do you choose to spend your time?

199. What values are being expressed when you do this?

200. What action would be aligned with your vision of you?

201. What is really important as you make this choice?

202. Where do you get caught in trivialities?

203. Where are you trapped in action?

204. What is significant about the choice you are making?

205. What is the central issue here?

206. How does it relate to who you are?

207. What will be the consequences of not paying attention to what really matters to you?

208. Will this matter to you 5 / 10 years from now?

209. What could you do that will matter?

210. If you were not in your current profession, what job would you love?

211. What job would you hate?

212. What is your favourite swear word?

213. What causes you to use it?
214. What is your favourite sound?
215. Where does that sound take you?
216. If you were stranded on a desert island, what book would you take with you?
217. Which contemporary person would you take with you?
218. Which historical person would you take with you?
219. If you could meet anyone in history, who would it be?
220. What do you imagine you could spend a solid week doing without getting bored?
221. What do you strive most for in your life: security, love, power, excitement, knowledge or something else?
222. If you could be a champion at some sport, which one would you choose?
223. What kind of champion would you be?
224. What would be a perfect weekend for you?
225. What is your most treasured memory?
226. What is the age range of your friends and what does that tell you??
227. What is one long-term goal of yours that has been achieved?
228. What are you grateful for in your life?
229. When did you last yell at someone?
230. What made you yell?
231. Do you consider spending time alone?
232. How would you feel comfortable about going to dinner or a show alone?
233. How would you feel asking for help?
234. When do you feel comfortable asking for help?
235. If you were famous, what would you like to be famous for?

236. What have you dreamed of doing?

237. What would make you compulsive about something?

238. How close is your family?

239. What do you do to honour those relationships?

240. Who is the most important person in your life?

241. What do you most value in a relationship?

Chapter 11
Work and Life Balance

Contents

Being in the Zone

> This section helps your client explore being in balance or
> flow with themselves and the environment around them.
> This enables them to learn how to be in their most
> productive zone.

1. When do you know you are in your flow?

2. What changes your flow?

3. How could you get more in tune with yourself?

4. What does flow / balance mean to you?

5. How is balance in your life right now?

6. What things are you doing that you would like to stop
    doing or delegate to someone else?

7. How do you know when you are being fully present?

8. When is your work and life truly in the zone?

9. What is the impact on those around you?

10. What did they notice that was different?

11. How could you re-create it at will in the future?

12. How are you living your most important values now, in the present?

13. What would believing you can live a perfect life do for you?

14. When is life perfect for you?

15. What are you seeing, hearing and feeling when life is good for you?

16. What would make it even better?

17. What changes do you need to make?

18. How are you going to make those changes?

19. What would be different?

20. Who do you know who has their work / life balanced?

21. What do they do differently?

22. What could you learn from them?

23. What would it be like to live a day in their shoes?

24. What do you think they would say having spent a day in your shoes?

25. What do you think they could learn from you?

26. When did you last do something just for you?

27. What are you not getting enough of?

28. What are you getting too much of?

29. What would encourage you to seek more balance?

30. How do you allow external factors to affect your ability to stay in your zone?

Commitment

Questions to evaluate your clients desire to achieve their stated goals and outcomes in relation to their work and life balance.

31. What are your top commitments?

32. What made them your top commitments?

33. What do you do to honour them?

34. What do you notice about them?

35. What gets in your way of delivering some / all of your commitments?

36. If you were to rate them on a scale of 1 – 10, how much of an impact do they have on your work / life balance?

37. What have you given up on?

38. What caused you to let them go?

39. Where do you need to put energy, focus and attention?

40. How could you be more energised / focused / attentive?

41. What do you miss?

42. What would having the missing bits do for you?

43. What did they give you in the past?

44. What enabled you to persevere in the past?

45. How can you get or recreate those feelings of commitment / perseverance?

46. How would having those feelings help you to move forward?

47. How important is commitment to you in your life / work?

48. How important is your commitment to your family / team / organisation?

49. What would a 100% life / job look, sound and feel like?

50. When do you know you are listening / listened to 100%?

51. What enables you to be / give 100%

52. What drives you?

53. How do you expect others to commit to you?

54. What enables you to truly commit?

55. What support do you require?

56. When have you fully committed to something?

57. What did that feel like?

Future Planning

These are questions to stimulate the client's future. To enable them to get on their chosen pathway with a realistic action plan.

58. What is possible?
59. What if it works out exactly as you want it to be?
60. What is the dream?
61. What is exciting to you about this?
62. What is the urge?
63. What does your intuition tell you?
64. What is the action plan?
65. What will you have to do to get the task done?
66. What support do you need to accomplish it?
67. What will you do?
68. When will you do it?
69. What will you take away from this?
70. How do you explain this to yourself?
71. What was the lesson?
72. How can you make sure you remember what you have learned?
73. How could you pull all this together?
74. How would you summarise your effort so far?
75. What action will you take?
76. Is this a time for action?
77. Where do you go from here?
78. When will you do that?
79. What are your next steps?
80. By what date or time will you complete these steps?
81. What would happen if you did nothing?
82. When did you decide that?

83. How did you decide that?

84. What is the current situation?

85. If you could take one option that you believe would add most value, what would it be?

86. What will that do for you?

87. When you think years into the future what will be the cost of either choice?

88. How will you maintain balance as you take action?

Habits

This section helps the client to identify certain repeating behaviour patterns that already exist and identify new patterns that would be a welcome addition to their lives.

89. What great habits do you already have that you can build upon?

90. If you could imagine some useful new habits what would they be?

91. If you started doing them what could they do for you?

92. What would need to happen to enable you to keep them?

93. What could blow you off course?

94. How long do you think it would take to become a habit?

95. What needs to happen for it to be sustainable?

96. So, you used to do 'X' 'Y' and 'Z' - what did that do for you? [note to coach 'X' 'Y' & 'Z' = listing their old habits]

97. What changed to stop you from doing that?

98. When you think of having 'X' 'Y' and 'Z' back, what would that do for you?

99. What do you want to do now, that you will do each day to balance the life you want?

100. Is that manageable for you?

101. How are your habitual behaviours impacting on what you now want?

102. When you think of the habits you have, what do they do for you?

103. What would a chart to track them look like?

104. What would happen if you were to monitor each of your new habits?

105. What would happen if you took 5 minutes out every couple of hours to practice some new habits?

106. What do you notice as you slow your pace?

107. What would happen if you turned your mobile and email off for a few hours?

108. What could you include in your daily habits that would feel like an indulgence?

109. What do you love doing?

110. When can you find time to do it?

111. How are your current habits consistent with your values?

112. What habit do you have which you would like to get rid of?

113. What will you do to interrupt this habit?

114. What habit could you develop which would support your goals?

Personal History

This section of personal history questions enables the coach and the client to explore thinking and feelings around the client's current pace and activities. Can also be used near the beginning of the coaching relationship (see also page 8).

115. How do you create stress through your thinking habits?

116. When do you confuse thought with fact?

117. How realistic are your thinking processes?
118. What would happen if you took more than one perspective on the situation?
119. What other choice could you make?
120. How could you slow down / speed up?
121. What activities or thoughts encourage a sense of peacefulness for you?
122. What is positive about the pace you are living at?
123. What is the cost to you and your friends and family of maintaining this pace?
124. What internal voices lead you to anxiety and overwhelm?
125. How would you describe them?
126. How could you change them?
127. Where would you like a different balance in your life?
128. How would you like it to be?
129. What does work / life balance mean to you?
130. Where do the boundaries lie for you between the company and you as an individual?
131. What issues are important to you when considering work / life balance?
132. What motivates you?
133. What metaphor would describe you to date?

Reflections

These questions enable the client to notice and carefully consider where they are and where they want to be. Useful information for moving forward can be generated by asking these questions.

134. What causes you to have a reflective period of time?
135. How do you choose to spend your time?

136. What actions will bring your vision into your daily life?
137. What can you do this year to live your values?
138. What is it like when you 'play' at full strength?
139. What do you need to let go of in order to be back in the flow?
140. What moved you out of your flow?
141. How could you participate in a different way?
142. What would be the benefits?
143. How do you suppose you could improve the situation?
144. What could you do differently?
145. What is your conclusion?
146. How would you describe this reflecting back?
147. What do you think this all amounts to?
148. What is the basic tension here?
149. What is funny about this situation?
150. If you were looking for the humour what would you find?
151. What would it feel like to have a good laugh about this?
152. How do you want things to be different?
153. What are you doing now to change?
154. What are you not doing now?
155. What would you like to do differently compared to before?
156. What skills would you like to acquire?
157. What is important now and how is this reflected in your life?
158. How comfortable are you with yourself?
159. How is the life you're living now worth what you're giving up in order to have it?
160. What do your reflections of life mean?
161. What does it feel like?
162. What is the part that is not yet clear?

163. If you had a perfect day, what would you have done?

164. What is the best thing about getting out of bed in the morning?

Values

These questions elicit what is truly important to your client. They are unique to your client, the qualities that define them and help them make choices about their balance. Values relate to principles rather than morals and are why we do what we do.

165. What is important to you about work / life balance?

166. What is it about that that makes it important?

167. When did you decide that that was important to you?

168. What do you care about?

169. What annoys you?

170. What is it about that which causes you to feel that way?

171. When were your work and life truly in balance for you?

172. How was that working?

173. What were you doing to make it in balance?

174. Who else was it having an impact on?

175. What was the emotion that was happening at that time?

176. How could you create that balance again?

177. What actions are most aligned to your values?

178. What would be your top five values?

179. How much are you honouring those top five?

180. As you look at your most important values are they moving you towards or away from a more balanced life?

181. How have those top five values changed over time?

182. What influences these values?

183. How much do those values reflect who you are?

184. How do they show up in your day-to-day life?

185. How will you know the difference?

186. What is really at stake in living your values?

187. What is most important to you that you are neglecting?

188. How would living your values impact your work / life balance?

189. What additional values could help you achieve a more effective work life balance?

190. What do you notice when you pay attention to these additional values?

191. What would be the consequences of incorporating them into your life?

Voting 'YES' and 'NO'

This section explores choices made and what your client agrees to do or not do, according to how they vote with a 'YES' or 'NO' to help them maintain balance at all times.

192. How aware are you of the things you say 'YES' and 'NO' to that alter your balance?

193. What do you need to 'know' in order to decline something?

194. What do you notice when you have the ability to do the right thing for you by saying 'YES' or 'NO'?

195. To have time for what is really important, what will you say 'NO' to?

196. How could this skill serve you?

197. What would it say about you if you had this skill?

198. How do you want to create this skill?

199. What do you want to say 'YES' to in your life?

200. What do you want to say 'NO' to in your life?

201. What will you do differently and say 'NO' to in order to do the 'YES' things?

202. Do you have to do 'X' or do you want to do 'X'?

203. What would increase your wanting to?

204. Do you find it harder to neglect your family than to say 'NO' to your work?

205. What is the real cost of this?

206. By saying 'YES' to longer work hours, what are you saying 'NO' to?

207. What do you wish you had more time to do?

208. What are you holding onto when you cannot say 'NO'?

209. What state do requests put you in?

210. How could that state be changed?

211. Who do you know who is able to decline additional requests?

212. How do they handle these situations?

213. What could they teach you?

214. Where are you not being honest by agreeing or disagreeing?

215. What would you like to model in order to change what you do?

216. What would be the benefits of causing a change?

217. When can you start to practice?

218. Who will support you and champion this?

219. How does this impact those around you?

220. What would they want you to say 'YES' and 'NO' to?

221. How would that align with your choices?

222. What boundaries would need to be explained / set up?

223. How could you strengthen your resolve to make choices?

Voting Energy

It can be really useful to get your client to study their energy
patterns for a period of time, maybe paying particular attention
to their thoughts as well as actions before asking some of the
following questions.

224. What is the area that, if you made an improvement, would
     give you and others the greatest return on time, energy,
     and money invested?
225. What do you concentrate on?
226. What do you need to do to be at peace?
227. How are you thinking about your problems?
228. How could you think differently?
229. How are you limiting your choices by these thoughts?
230. What other perspective could you take?
231. How are you indulging in self-created suffering with this
     train of thought?
232. What different story could you create about this situation?
233. How could you think of this as fun or easy?
234. How could your thoughts serve you in this circumstance?
235. How could you lighten up on yourself?
236. When are you alert and have effortless control?
237. What was happening?
238. What can you change to get in the flow?
239. How do you want to chart your incremental progress?
240. From where do you get most of your energy?
241. When are you at your lowest / highest energy points?
242. How can you preserve your energy?
243. What sustains you?

Voting Finances

Questions to explore how your client votes with their money – do they make the choices they really want to make?

244. How do you want to vote with your money?
245. What / who do you wish to support with your money?
246. How do you make choices about how to spend your money?
247. How will you decide a product / service is worth what you spend on it?
248. What are your criteria for selecting goods?
249. How much is enough?
250. How much of your time and energy are you willing to trade for money?
251. What do you really believe about how you spend your money?
252. How is this aligned with your values?
253. How do you benefit from your choices? What is abundance?
254. What really matters to you about money?
255. Where do you get your greatest value from?
256. What specific behaviours will honour your intentions?
257. How will your life be different if you vote in this way?
258. What message are you sending by voting in this way?
259. What difference do you want to make by voting in this way?
260. If you had more than enough money for your needs how would you spend the rest?
261. How would that make you feel?

My Favourite Questions

Chapter 12
Lifestyle and Wellness

Contents

Fitness

> Being physically and mentally fit and healthy is important for every aspect of life. Being able to perform and maintain physical activity is vital in every aspect to their well-being. These questions challenge, encourage and motivate.

1.　How balanced are you physically, on a scale of 1 – 10?

2.　How often do you exercise?

3.　What does fitness mean for you?

4.　How fit would you say you are?　On a scale of 1 – 10?

5.　How fit do you want to be?

6.　What would it mean to you to be fitter?

7.　How fit would you like to be? On a scale of 1 – 10?

8.　What needs to change to make it a 10?

9.　What must you become conscious of in your life in order to overcome inertia?

10.　What fitness goals do you have?

11.　To what extent do you achieve your fitness goals?

12.　What stops you from achieving your fitness goals?

13.　How fit do you want to be?

14.　What would that look/sound/feel like?

15. What challenges do you continue to face in achieving your fitness goals?

16. How is your energy at the moment? On a scale of 1 – 10?

17. What could make it a 10?

18. What would it be like to have that?

19. What impact on your life would having energy at the ten level have?

20. How sustainable is that?

21. How do you know this is something you really want?

22. Who says it is worth it for you?

23. What would you have to give up in order to sustain your new energy level?

24. What would you have to continue doing to maintain that level?

25. Who are you being with your current lifestyle?

26. Who would you become if you became fitter?

27. What would others say about you if you made the changes you want to?

28. What kind of resources would assist you?

29. What do you need to do in order to generate what you need?

30. How are you getting in your own way?

31. What needs to be moved to allow you to drive forwards towards your goals?

32. What would be your first three steps to achievement?

33. Who are your cheerleaders?

34. What do you want from them?

35. How will you ask for what you want?

36. When will you ask them?

37. What would be your motivation to start the journey to greater fitness?

38. What would you need to do to maintain your motivation when it gets difficult?

39. What other sources of inspiration are available to you?

40. When you wake up tomorrow, what will you do that ensures you begin this journey?

Health

This section helps your client explore being in balance and sound in body, mind and spirit.

41. How do you take care of yourself?

42. What would you like to do, be, have?

43. What health challenges do you currently face?

44. What could you do about them?

45. When will you address all the issues?

46. What assistance do you need?

47. What would assist you to begin dealing with them?

48. What is your body saying to you now?

49. What action will you take to respond positively?

50. If you did take action...what would your body say about it?

51. What could you do differently?

52. And what impact on your wellbeing could that have?

53. What input do you have into sustaining a healthy life?

54. How could you affect how healthy you are?

55. What do you want to change about your health?

56. What would happen if you did?

57. What action can you take now that would have an immediate impact?

58. What are you willing to give up to make positive changes?
59. What are you willing to start to make a positive change to how you feel?
60. How many times have you tried to make a change?
61. What will be different this time?
62. Who or what can support your efforts?
63. How will you know you are getting the results you want?
64. What gets in your way to making a change?
65. What would be the first thing to eliminate?
66. What would be the first thing to add?
67. When will you make changes if not now?
68. How big does the change need to be to make a start?
69. What do you need to do to mitigate sabotaging yourself?
70. What activities would be most engaging and sustaining?
71. What are your options?
72. What are the benefits of these options?
73. What are the effects that would most benefit you?
74. When will you be ready to commit?
75. How can I best serve you in your new endeavours?
76. What is a simple first step?
77. If, that step was taken, what next?
78. What part of you will cause most resistance?
79. What do you need to say or do with that part?
80. What rewards do you envisage as you achieve your goals?
81. What do you perceive threatens your health?
82. When will you take a break today?
83. What is it to be generous with yourself today?
84. What does being healthy mean to you?
85. What does being healthy feel like?
86. What does being healthy sound like?

Mindfulness

This section helps your client focus. Mindfulness is paying attention on purpose, in the present moment and in a non-judgmental way. It can often be accomplished through forms of meditation or focus on one's breathing.

87.   What does being mindful mean to you?

88.   What would it be like for you if you spent more time 'being' than 'doing'?

89.   What does mindfulness mean to you?

90.   Where is your energy focused right now?

91.   How often do you pay attention to your breathing?

92.   When you focus on your breathing; how is it?

93.   What is your breathing like?

94.   How mindful are you in your life?

95.   How are you feeling right now?

96.   What needs to change?

97.   What do you want to change?

98.   How will you begin that change?

99.   What resources will be required for you to start and maintain the change?

100. What do you feel you ought/must/should change?

101. Who says and what do you say?

102. When/where in your life do you go slow/slow down?

103. How do you conserve your energy?

104. What delights you?

105. Where do you find peace?

106. How often do you go inside yourself to find the answer?

107. How often do you go inside yourself to find inner peace?

108. How often do you go inside yourself to find balance?

109. How often/when do you focus on what your body is telling you?
110. What is your body telling you right now?
111. How balanced is your life?
112. Where do you notice imbalance?
113. Where do you notice most balance?
114. What does balance feel like for you?
115. Where in your life do you need rebalancing?
116. If there was greater balance what would be different?
117. What would you need to do to feel a greater sense of balance?
118. What stops you addressing this?
119. How can you remove one small barrier at a time?
120. What would happen if you did?
121. How balanced are you mentally, on a scale of 1 – 10?
122. What would be happening if the score was 10?
123. How often do you practice just being quiet and concentrating on your being?
124. Where do you sense your connection with the ground?
125. How can you connect more often?
126. What would change if you were to become more mindful?
127. How would you be if you were to become successful at mindfulness?
128. What activities do you notice you enjoy the most?
129. What do you notice when you are still and quiet?
130. How could you eat in a mindful way?
131. What changes would you need to bring to your mealtimes to enable mindful eating?
132. What changes would be required to enable you to connect with your family / colleagues in a mindful way?

Resilience

These questions refer to investigating your client's action of making low-priority tasks more important than high-priority ones. Exploring what causes the putting off of important tasks and your client's strategy for avoidance.

384. If the issue wasn't there to keep you busy, what would be?
385. What keeps you awake at night?
386. What could you differently at the time that you awake?
387. Who are you without the stress?
388. What thoughts / memories do you have when you feel totally calm and relaxed?
389. What top three things specifically make you anxious?
390. What top five things relax you?
391. How much personal time, per week, can you invest in ensuring anxiety or stress does not dominate your life?
392. What could you differently at the time that you awake?
393. Who are you without the stress?
394. What thoughts / memories do you have when you feel totally calm and relaxed?
395. What top three things specifically make you anxious?
396. What top five things relax you?
397. How much personal time, per week, can you invest in ensuring anxiety or stress does not dominate your life?
398. How will you treat yourself well?
399. What is it like for you to be really present?
400. How can you be really present with what is keeping you awake at night?
401. When you are really present with the issue how does it change your perception of it?

402. What do you perceive causes you stress?

403. Who owns that?

404. What resources do you already have to help you manage stress?

405. How resilient are you?

406. On a scale of 1 - 10?

407. What changes your resilience?

408. When you are at your most resilient how does that feel?

409. Where do you give your power away?

410. Who do you give your power to?

411. When do you give your power away?

412. What top three things nourish you?

413. What will recharge your batteries?

414. What practices could anchor you in the here and now?

415. How are you choosing to be in this moment?

416. What other choices do you have?

417. What are you feeling 'out of control' of?

418. What can you/can't you control right now?

419. If you were conductor of an orchestra - who are you conducting?

420. Who is playing out of tune?

421. Who are you choosing to be?

422. What are you choosing to see/not see?

423. What are you avoiding?

424. What are you choosing to do/not do?

425. How do you want to see this situation?

426. Which way are you going to choose to see this situation?

427. How do you want to be in relation to this situation?

428. How are you going to choose to be in this situation?

429. So, how far outside your comfort zone are you?

430. How could you stretch your comfort zone?

431. How far do you want to stretch your comfort zone?

432. Where does it need stretching?

433. If you could encompass this situation within your comfort zone how would that be for you?

434. What symptoms of stress are you experiencing?

435. What are the warning signs that you are becoming stressed?

436. What are the warning signs that you are already feeling stressed?

437. How could you manage them?

438. What do you notice?

439. What needs to change?

440. Where is this feeling of stress coming from?

441. Whose issue is this?

442. What sort of gap is there between feeling stressed and feeling resilient?

443. Instead of should/must/ought how would changing your language to 'would like to have' change how you feel?

444. How is where you focus your energy matching your values?

445. What pressure are you currently putting yourself under?

446. How could you relieve that pressure?

447. What can you do about this right now?

448. Is this the right time to be worrying about that?

449. Where are you holding your tension?

450. Focus on it then relax - how does that feel?

451. Where do you feel most relaxed?

452. Where is your relaxing place?

453. What is relaxing about that place?

454. Can you take yourself to that place now?

455. Could you take yourself to that relaxing place in the future?

456. What will recharge your batteries?

457. How can you contribute to your reserves of fun / balance / resourcefulness?

458. What do you do that builds your resilience?

459. What could you do that would increase your resilience?

460. What would be a simple strategy for changing your state when required?

461. What could you do that would ensure you have a resourceful state?

Weight Loss

These questions relate to supporting your client to become more conscious of what they want to achieve and helping them focus on the means to achieve a healthy attitude and motivation to weight loss.

133. What is your relationship with food?

134. What challenges do you face in maintaining your weight loss?

135. Who can support you in this?

136. How committed are you to maintaining your weight loss?

137. What do you notice when you eat?

138. Where are you when you eat your meals?

139. How consciously are you eating?

140. How many times do you chew your food?

141. How do you know when you are hungry?

142. How do you know when you are full?

143. What types of food are you most attracted to?

144. What are they doing for you?
145. How much exercise do you do?
146. How often do you exercise?
147. What type of exercise really gets your heart pumping?
148. What type of exercise do you enjoy?
149. What small changes could you make to your daily exercise routine?
150. What small changes could you make in your life that will support you in your weight loss journey?
151. How do you know when to stop eating?
152. How do you know when it is time to eat?
153. How do you view food?
154. Tell me something about your mealtimes.
155. What do you say Yes/No to when you are out shopping?
156. What are five reasons you want to lose weight?
157. How will you feel better when you lose weight?
158. What will you see when you lose weight?
159. What will you hear when you lose weight?
160. How will life be better because you were successful?
161. What behaviours do you recognise as sabotaging?
162. Where could the first change in a behaviour take place?
163. What would happen if that change took place?
164. What makes you think you are ready to make changes?
165. What behaviours to do you have that support your weight loss?
166. What can you add to those?
167. What habits need to be altered?
168. What roadblocks do you envision?
169. What contingencies can you put in place?
170. Who can support you?

171. How will you do that?

172. How could you record / chart the changes you want to make?

173. Where have you broken bad habits in the past?

174. What would you need to do to adopt a similar strategy now?

175. What keeps you from making small changes?

176. How would things have to change for you to do somethings differently?

177. What can you try differently when you feel hungry late at night etc.?

178. What were you thinking when you came off your planned eating plan?

179. How did it serve you?

180. How can you remind yourself what your plan is?

181. How can you remind yourself to drink more water?

182. What would be an easier way of having the right food available when you need it?

183. What will you do if you get hungry after lunch?

184. When will you fit the two-mile walk into your schedule?

185. What would work best for you?

186. How will change your schedule to allow room for the changes?

187. What would it take to put new practices in place when you eat?

188. How can you make this new way joyful?

189. What things are most important to you?

190. How does your exercise and eating fit into this?

191. What sorts of things would you like to accomplish in your life?

192. What would you like to see change?
193. If things were better with your eating/exercise, what would be different?
194. What have you already tried?
195. What worked?
196. What didn't work?'
197. Imagine you can make the changes easily, what did you do?
198. Imagine you are already have the weight loss, what do you see / hear / feel?
199. Imagine that you have the body and health you desire. What did it take for you to achieve it?
200. When were you successful with changing in the past?
201. How could you do more of that?
202. In what ways does this concern you?
203. If you decided to make a change, what makes you think you could do it?
204. How would you like things to be different?
205. How would things be better if you changed?
206. What concerns you now about your current exercise and eating patterns?
207. If you decided to change, on a scale of 1-10, how confident are you that you could change
208. What small, manageable steps could you undertake now?
209. If not now, when?
210. What would need to happen first?
211. What might get in your way?
212. What do you think you will do next?
213. What is next for you?

214. What do you see happening in five years if you do not make changes?

215. If you decide to change, what will it be like?

216. How would you like things to be different?

217. What is good about 'X' behavior [where 'X' behavior is the problem behavior they want to change]?

218. What is BAD about changing? What would you lose or give up if you got rid of 'X'?

219. if you were the coach, what would you recommend?

220. What results do you hope to obtain? What else?

221. What distance exists between the results you hope to obtain and your current location? What else?

222. What is the best you can do to obtain the results you want?

223. What else can you do?

224. What would you do if you had no limits?

225. What else is there with no limits?

226. What is stopping you from getting the results you want?

227. What can you do to minimise or overcome these obstacles?

228. What else can you do to overcome / minimise?

229. What are you willing to do to achieve your goal?

230. On a scale of 1 to 10, what is the degree of commitment you have for your goal?

231. What do I really want to achieve?

232. What will you do to achieve it?

233. What will you do that depends on you to reach your goal?

234. What else can assist you?

235. What will others perceive about you when you achieve your goal?

236. How will achieving your goal affect other parts of your life?

237. What do you need to reach your goal?

238. When was the last time you were addicted to being right?

239. What was happening at that time?

240. What would you do differently next time you were in a similar situation?

241. How satisfied are you with your life nowadays?

242. What extent do you feel the things you do in your life are worthwhile?

243. How happy did you feel yesterday?

244. How anxious did you feel yesterday?

My Favourite Questions

Addendum
Get Out of Jail!

> This section has been created for those exceptionally 'sticky' moments. The moments when all words and thoughts fail you! These questions allow you to gain further insight and generate the space that can enable you to subsequently find the right question at the right moment. Trust what comes!

1. What is next?
2. What do you want?
3. What do you really want?
4. What else?
5. What is here, right now for you?
6. When will that happen?
7. What is the first step?
8. What would you like more of / less of?
9. What gets in the way?
10. What else might you do?
11. What should you do?
12. When will you start?
13. If not you, then who?
14. If not now, then when?
15. What can you do differently?
16. What could you do today?
17. What more can you tell me?
18. What stops you?
19. What would be a stretch for you?
20. Whose voice is it?
21. How is it working for you?

22. What would that do for you?
23. What did you notice?
24. What inspires you?
25. Who are you being?
26. Who is in control?
27. What is mastery in this area?
28. What is really important to you?
29. How did you show up today?
30. How are you showing up right now?
31. Can we go there in more detail?
32. What is the central issue here?
33. What do you want for yourself?
34. Who are you becoming?
35. What is the cost to you of playing safe?
36. If you couldn't fail, what would you do?
37. How do you want it to be?
38. What is it to be present?
39. What is choice?
40. What should I ask you now?
41. What possibilities come to mind?
42. So, what works for you?
43. What was your part in that?
44. If the worse happened, what would the silver lining be?
45. What else could you do?
46. What does this mean for you?
47. When is enough, enough?
48. What do you care about?
49. What is holding you back?
50. What is 'good enough' for right now?

Publications

Between us we have read many books on the subject of coaching, here is just a selection.

Blakey, John (2016). **The Trusted Executive**: Nine Leadership Habits that Inspire Results, Relationships & Reputation. Kogan Page.

Blakey, John & Day, Ian (2012). **Challenging Coaching** Going beyond traditional coaching to face the FACTS. Nicholas Brealey.

Barber, Judy (2005). **Good Question!** The art of asking questions to bring about positive change. Bookshaker.

Cairns, Margot (1998). **Approaching the Corporate Heart.** Simon & Schuster.

Carlson, Richard (1993). **Stop Thinking & Start Living.** Thorson.

Charvet, Shelle Rose (1997). **Words That Change Minds.** Mastering the Language of Influence by. Kendall/Hunt

Clutterbuck, David with David Megginson (2006). **Making Coaching Work.** CIPD

Covey, Stephen R. (2004). **The 7 Habits of Highly Effective People.** Simon & Schuster.

Downey, Myles (2003). **Effective Coaching** Lessons from the Coach's coach. Thomson.

Elfline, Jan (2009). **Quotes to Inspire, Questions to Inquire** coaching cards. www.janelfline.com

Forster, Mark (2006). **Do It Tomorrow** and other secrets of time management. Hodder & Stoughton.

Gallwey, W. Timothy (1997). **The Inner Game of Tennis**. Random House

Grant, Wendy (1997). **Resolving Conflicts** how to turn Conflict into Cooperation. Vega.

Hall Ph.D, L. Michael with Michelle Duval, Master Coach (2005). **Meta-Coaching Vol II Coaching Conversations for Transformational Change.** Neuro-Semantic Publications.

Jeffers, Susan (2003). **Embracing Uncertainty** Achieving peace of mind as we face the unknown. Hodder Mobius.

Jeffers, Susan (1997). **Feel the Fear and Do it Anyway**. Rider & Co.

Kline, Nancy (1999). **Time to Think:** Listening to Ignite the Human Mind. Cassell.

Kline, Nancy (2015). **More Time to Think:** The Power of Independent Thinking. Cassell.

Kohlrieser, George (2006). **Hostage at the Table** how leaders overcome conflict, influence others & raise performance. Wiley.

Kotter, John with Holger Rathgeber (2006). **Our Iceberg is Melting** Changing and Succeeding Under Any Conditions. Pan Macmillan.

McMahon, Gladeana with Anne Archer – edited by (2010). **101 Coaching Strategies and Techniques**. Routledge

Mackay, Ian (1995). **Asking Questions**. IPD

Marquardt, Michael (2005). **Leading with Questions**. Jossey-Bass

Molden, David (2001). **NLP Business Masterclass**. Prentice Hall (Financial Times)

O'Connell, Fergus (2005). **How To Do A Great Job And Go Home On Time.** Pearson Prentice Hall.

O'Connor, Joseph with Andrea Lages (2004). **Coaching with NLP**. Element

O'Connor, Joseph with Andrea Lages (2007). **How Coaching Works.** A & C Black.

O'Connor, Joseph with Ian McDermott (2001). **Way of NLP.** Thorsons.

O'Neill, Mary Beth (2000). **Executive Coaching with Backbone and Heart.** Wiley.

Parashar, Fiona (2003). **The Balancing Act** Work-Life Solutions for Busy People. Simon & Schuster.

Rogers, Jenny (2004). **Coaching Skills** a handbook. Open University Press.

Scott, Susan (2002). **Fierce Conversations.** Piatkus.

Scoular, Anne (2011) **The Financial Times Guide to Business Coaching.** Published by FT Prentice Hall.

Their, Marian J (2003). **Coaching Clues:** Real Stories, Powerful Solutions, Practical Tools. Nicholas Brealey.

Thich Nhat Hanh & Dr Lilian Cheung, (2015) **Mindful Eating, Mindful Life**. Hay House.

Whitmore, John (2002). **Coaching for Performance** Growing People, Performance and Purpose. Nicholas Brealey Publishing

Whitworth Laura, with Karen Kimsey-House, Henry Kimsey-House, Philip Sandall (2009). **Co-Active Coaching**. Davies-Black (Nicholas Brealey)

Further Information

If you would like to find out more about coaching, accredited training and coaching competencies, the following, on this page and the next, are very good starting points:

International Coach Federation (ICF)

www.coachfederation.org

2365 Harrodsburg RD, Suite A325

Lexington

Kentucky

40504

USA

International Coach Federation (UK Chapter)

www.coachfederation.org.uk

59 Birmingham Road,

Lichfield,

Staffordshire

WS13 6PG

Academy of Executive Coaching Ltd (AoEC)

www.aoec.com

8 Northumberland Avenue,

London,

WC2N 5BY

Association for Coaching (AC)

www.associationforcoaching.com

Golden Cross House,

8 Duncannon Street,

London

WC2N 4JF

European Coaching & Mentoring Council (EMCC)

www.emccouncil.org

PO Box 3154

Marlborough,

Wiltshire, SN8 3WD